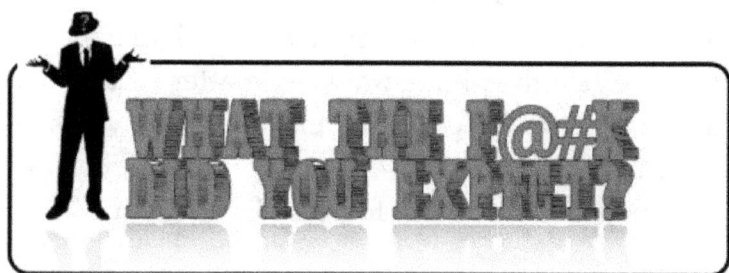
WHAT THE F@#K DID YOU EXPECT?

"When shit hits the fan, is you still a fan?
When shit hits the fan, is you still a fan?
Want you look to your left and right,
make sure you ask your friends.
When shit hits the fan, is you still a fan?"

Mortal Man – Kendrick Lamar

This is dedicated to the ones who never leave me. When I act a fool, or lose my way, you still believe in me. When the phone rings, no matter what, you always answer. Doesn't matter the days or years that may go by. Whenever I ask you to roll, you always say let's ride. And for that, I thank you.

M. Andre'

WHAT THE F@#K DID YOU EXPECT?

AN *uncensored* GUIDE TO MEN, WOMEN, AND THEIR RELATIONSHIPS

by André Kali

LEGEND

Legend Enterprises

ISBN: 9780692475843

Table of Contents

Introduction

If you pay attention, you just might learn some-thing.

Have you ever wondered what makes rela-tionships so complicated? Why can they be so frus-trating and difficult to navigate? Why is she trip-pin'? Why is he trippin'? And since you can't figure it out, you find yourself just shaking your head and saying shit like, "it is what it is." Well, if you are re-ally interested in exactly what "it" is, then this guide is for you. You see "it" isn't what it is. "It" is either what you make of it or what you allow it to become. Most of us have no idea how to make relationships work. Hell, most folks struggle to find a person to attempt a relationship with in the first place. If you want to know why, it's because this isn't high school anymore. Passing notes in homeroom and holding hands in the hallway is child's play, so any child can do that. However, when you finally grow up, life has a funny way of changing the game. For example, when you're 17, you're cool with your boyfriend living in his parent's basement. Now how does that shit work for you when you're 30? You liked talking to her on the phone until late in the night when you were 16. Now how much talking are you trying to listen to at 40? Exactly! That's why you need a guide, and that's why I wrote this book.

Let me start by telling you the truth: every relationship is a pain in the ass. Granted, some are definitely more painful than others, but they all are a pain in the ass. In my opinion, for what it's worth, (which, by the way, is exactly equal to the amount of money you paid for this book. My family thanks you) I don't believe there is any such thing as an expert on relationships. Relationships are facets of life, and like life, relationships are precious, fleeting, and unpredictable. It is believed in eastern spirituality that life's greatest achievement is enlightenment. So this guide seeks to enlighten you about men, women, and relationships.

Interestingly enough, how most people see their lives is completely determined by their relationships or lack thereof in certain cases. Countless people fully believe that because their relationships are miserable, that their lives suck. . . And they are correct! Nahhhhhhh, I'm only kidding, well partially kidding. No worries though, this is not a book about how loving yourself is the first step to being loved. My grandma used to warn that I would go blind for loving myself. Thank God that wasn't true. Don't worry, I washed my hands before I wrote the book. This is, however, a book of enlightenment. I decided to write this book as my way of shedding a little light on relationships, based on my own personal observations and failures with relationships. What I see as truths of omniscience, my philosophical father calls "paying attention to shit". Paying attention is one of the most important skills you can have in life, and particularly essential for your relationship success.

I know at this point many of you might be thinking that paying attention is simple. Why do you have to read an entire book about it? To that thinking I have two responses. First, there is an actual medical condition, ADHD, named from the fact that people have a deficit of the ability to pay attention. And B, you might want to consider that the reason that you don't want to read the entire book is because you have a problem paying attention. Furthermore, If you missed the fact that I started this thought with first, but finished with B, you're not fu@*kin paying attention.

How to read the guide.

You may have caught on from the introduction that this guide is written in a conversational tone. Don't be afraid. It is written that way to make our time together a little more personal. I should also prepare you for some of the language used within the guide. It is unsuitable for children! It is also not intended to be gratuitously vulgar. It is there because sometimes profane is more profound. It delivers a message in a way that punctuation alone cannot. More importantly, it really is just the way I would say it to you if we were having a conversation. Finally, there is Mr. Q.

Mr. Q is like the little man on my shoulder, adding his own comments to the conversation. When you see his symbol, *the text will change like this.* So you can tell when it's Mr. Q talking instead of me. There is no reason to be distracted or afraid, I'm pretty sure he doesn't bite.

Enjoy!

PART I

RELATIONSHIIPS 101

CHAPTER ONE

It's Not Rocket Science.

One of the first things we need to establish in regard to relationships are the rules of engagement. Sure, I understand that the term *rules of engagement* is usually meant for warfare, but relationships can result in about the same amount of carnage as war if you screw these things up enough. Besides, isn't war the ultimate sign of a failed relationship? I'm going to share with you what I see as the three different types of relationships that make up our daily lives. What's more valuable for you, is learning how to recognize and navigate through them effectively. This is a good time to get a highlighter because these will definitely be on the test at the end. Now different relationships have different rules, and these rules become more imperative to follow in correlation to the complexity of the relationship.

THE (non-relationship) RELATIONSHIP

Some relationships are so simple we don't even recognize them as relationships. They are the relationships we have within society. These relationships are important, if for nothing more than identifying psychopaths. I call it the non-relationship relationship because we don't really acknowledge them as relationships, but they really are. This rule deals with people you don't know and may never see again. This is the simplest of relationships and is tied to the Golden Rule "do unto others as you would have them do unto you." Saying "hi", showing a smile, or any number of random and simple acts of kindness costs you nothing, but can pay amazing dividends for you and your approach to life. Being nice generates positive energy; and being positive, makes you more attractive than being negative. People will like you, speak well of you and want to be around you. This is what is known as your likability factor. Your likability makes people more likely to do things for you and/or give you the benefit of the doubt when you make a mistake.

Unless your mistake is being black, and liking skittles, or playing loud music, or selling loose cigarettes, or stealing a cigar, or...you know what? Just try to be a little less black; it's safer.

What I will say for now, is that if you don't follow the Golden Rule in these situations it doesn't necessarily make you a bad person. You don't have to say "hi" or smile at anyone. However, it also doesn't make you someone who people will like, or someone for whom others would be willing to do something nice. So hey, if you are someone who has mastered self-sufficiency, or you wear a badge, then this approach may work for you. You probably haven't gained any enemies, but you sure as hell haven't gained any supporters either.

So what is the danger, right? Well, the danger comes from not just ignoring the rule, but violating it. Being an asshole to people, particularly those you don't even know, says a lot about your character, and it is not saying anything good. Really, how hard is it to say hello or just smile at someone when you make eye contact. It is a lot easier than pretending like people don't exist or are so beneath you that you need not acknowledge them. The danger is Karma, which is Hindi for payback is a bitch. Believe me; that shit will come back on you. It always does. Donald Trump's hair does not look like a nest forged by rabid pigeons with a crack addiction because he's a nice guy.

I had a co-worker at one point in my career that was pretty high ranking in the organization. For the purposes of this story, we will call her Lacey Kunt. Well, Ms. Kunt treated anyone and everyone who was not a VP or above like Marie Antoinette treated peasants. Furthermore, Ms. Kunt hated on the peasants so much that she used her influence to keep others from getting ahead. When a larger player acquired the company, nearly every executive found a home within the new organization. However, because no one had anything nice to say about that cunt, sorry I mean Ms. Kunt, she was not as fortunate. Karma is a bitch! Now I do realize that this reflective is a relationship with a co-worker and not a stranger, but I put it out there to make a point.

Many of our co-workers are merely habitual (non-relationship) relationships. You ride the elevator or pass in the hallways the same strangers every day. I'm talking about people whose names you don't even know after months of standing next to them at the coffee machine. I don't point this out to make you feel like an ass for never introducing yourself, but to illustrate that simply being familiar with someone, even if you do know their names and say hi every day, doesn't get you pass the non-relationship relationship. So always remember to follow the golden rule and for Christ's sake say "hi" to people. Now you might be asking, why should you care about a relationship with someone, when you may never see him or her again? That is a very good question, and I'm proud of you for coming up with it all on your own. Remember, there are no stupid questions, just questions being asked by stupid people.

THE PROFESSIONAL RELATIONSHIP

I realize that some readers may be wondering why a relationship with a co-worker is a non-relationship relationship instead of a professional relationship. It's actually a very good question. Understand that relationships are not about the setting of people, but the exchange between people. And since we are talking about exchange, welcome to the professional relationship. The professional relationship is founded on the win-win principle. This is the relationship where two people come together through a transaction for their mutual benefit. The entire interaction is based upon the exchange of an identified, and most often articulated, value. I am getting something from you, and in return, you are getting something from me. A simple example would be a man having relations with a prostitute. In exchange for her sexual services, the prostitute is remunerated in the form of a modest fee. Let me go on record to say that my assertion that the fee is modest is purely speculative and in no way an indication or admission of my knowledge of the fee schedule for the sexual services of a prostitute. In fact, let's just forget that I brought up that example altogether. However, if I could make one more point in my defense about that example, well actually two points. Prostitution is known as the world's oldest profession, and not by accident. Prostitutes are euphemistically referred to as working girls. Some people refer to prostitutes as ho's, but this is a complete mischaracterization. A ho, which is urban vernacular for a whore, is a woman who has sex, and a lot of it, without compensation. This by no means makes them bad people. Hell, I love me some ho's. It just means they decided that getting their education was more important than turning pro. Then you have freaks, which is really a completely different category. . . . . You know what, let's just move on.

Anyway, the rule for a professional relationship is "value for value." It is just that simple, I add value to you and in return, you add value to me. Warning! Do not confuse this with doing a favor or a solid. Those are tools used within another relationship type, and we will discuss that soon enough. Value for Value is generally an immediate transaction or net 30 at best. YOU DO NOT GET SOMETHING FOR NOTHING IN THE PROFESSIONAL RELATIONSHIP. Oh, and there's no sex in the champagne room either.. If you try to get something for nothing in a professional relationship, I can almost guarantee, *A Pimp Named Slipback will be going upside your mutha-@#*kin head for a little something he likes to call the principalities of restitution.

Just a side note for my white readers, there is no upside to this "upside", it simply denotes that you have just been forcefully struck about *the forehead region by a hand, most likely an open hand, that started from a region down around the ankles, gaining momentum and velocity as it works its way "up" and to the "side" of your aforementioned muthafu*#in head. *A Pimp Named Slipback is the full name, and you have to say the whole thing, it's like A Tribe Called Quest.*

THE PERSONAL RELATIONSHIP

There is a saying, "don't take it personally, it's only business". Appropriately, there probably isn't a better way to distinguish the stark contrast between the professional relationship and the personal relationship. You see in business it's all about the game, and just like there's no crying in baseball, there is a certain degree of detachment required to play the right way. Once we start to get attached, or more precisely feelings get involved, oh, its personal now muthf@#ka! Now we are getting to the good shit. The Personal Relationship is a relationship in which you share intimate information about yourself and your life with another person, and this person in turn shares intimate information with you. In my opinion, the personal relationship is the relationship sweet spot. The personal relationship is the relationship type that consistently offers the most bang for your buck. We reap the greatest benefits from our personal relationships because of two distinct paradigms that effectively mitigate, if not eliminate, any obligation of reciprocity. You can get something for nothing, directly, in return. Well, that is not exactly true. The reality is that you are leveraging the equity of your investment of intimacy. As a result, what you can receive is generally commensurate to what you have put in. If you are more comfortable with cliche', the rule of the personal relationship is "You reap what you sow."

As I mentioned, there are two paradigms I want to introduce. One I call "the familial effect of intimacy". The other is a term made famous by Ein-stien, with a little different interpretation, "the theo-ry of relativity". I guess geniuses do think alike. Let's talk about the theory of relativity first, since it is probably the easier concept to understand. The theory simply suggests that our closest personal re-lationships are with those people with whom we are related: parents, siblings, cousins, etc. Generally the closer the relation, the more personal it is. Therefore, in most cases you are closer to a sibling than you are to a cousin. Additionally, closeness can develop from proximity; literally the closer you are in dis-tance the closer you can potentially become person-ally. Now may be a good time to clear up some-thing. I don't want to confuse anyone that a person-al relationship actually means that people get along. . . It doesn't! It just means that you share intimate details of each other's lives, or some aspect of your respective lives. In fact, some people distance themselves from individuals, especially family, simply because that person may know a little too much about them, and be a little too willing to share it with others. For example, my brother has very little hesitation to bring up to people I introduce him to, that I wet the bed until I was seven. This isn't even entirely true. Well at least in the way it initially sounds. The truth is, at age seven, I was less concerned about avoiding a wet spot on the bed, than walking down the long dark hallway in the middle of the night. So my problem was more bogey man, than bladder. My mom and I had a heart to heart conversation one day; she bought a night-lite for the hallway and another for the bathroom...problem solved. My mom is nice like that, but I digress. What the theory of relativity comes comes down to is, there are people who have borne witness to your life. They have watched nearly everything you have done and know more details about you than almost any other person will ever learn. That is what makes the relationship extremely personal. Unfortunately, it's that way, whether you like them or not. Hey, you can't choose your relatives. If you could, a few cousins and at least one sibling would be dropping like flies. (No no, not you, him. You know you're my favorite.)

The other paradigm is similar, but nuanced: the *familial effect of intimacy*. Sounds fancy, but it really is just the result of sharing intimate information with another person with whom you are not related. This exchange, almost without exception, immediately makes any two people closer to one another. How close people become depends upon the frequency, length, or depth of their interactions, proximity, and the resulting exchange or sharing of intimate experiences. This explains why many of our friendships develop from the time we spend with others at school, at work, or at some other regularly scheduled social activity. For example, our first friends are the kids from the neighborhood. Then we start attending school, and our friends are drawn from classmates and so on. Being in close proximity with someone, every day, over a period of time, presents more opportunities to share intimate experiences and information about ourselves, as a result we forge personal relationships. Many of us have friends who are like a brother or sister to us, perhaps a friend's mom or dad, that you call mom or dad because you, and their actually child are so close. We actually forge bonds that are so close that we categorized them as being familial or "like family", hence the familial effect.

Whew! I'm glad he explained that. For a minute I thought the familial effect was something you catch, like chlamydia"

So there you have it, well at least as I see it, the three distinct types of relationships with three simple, but specific rules of engagement.

The (Non-relationship) Relationship: just follow the Golden Rule of "do unto others as you would have them do unto you." Would it kill your ass to smile and acknowledge your fellow man? The Professional Relationship: It's about Value for Value. Therefore, try not to get so excited about what you stand to gain, until you understand what is expected from you in return. You don't get anything for free. There may not be a fee, but there is always a cost. Last, but most definitely not the least, The Personal Relationship: you reap what you sow. You have to invest your part of who you are into the relationship in return for part of someone else. Remember intimacy = vulnerability, and people take that shit personally. Now you can identify your relationships and apply the rules in order to be more effective in navigating your interactions. I realize that it won't always be as easy as I have made it seem; life never is, but I can at least guarantee you this; it's not rocket science.

CHAPTER TWO

*So Now You're Fu#*ing Wit Me*

When I recapped the distinct relationship types (the non-relationship relationship, the professional relationship, and the personal relationship), I said that the personal relationship was last, but was most definitely not the least of the three relationships covered. Let me explain what I mean by that statement. The personal relationship is at the top of the relationship hierarchy. I'm not suggesting that you make it a goal, but it is the pinnacle of relationships, which makes personal relationships simultaneously the most rewarding and costly relationship in which you can be engaged. Here is an important fact: all personal relationships are intimate relationships. Intimacy is, by its nature, an emotional construct. Meaning that intimacy is all about feelings, nothing more than feelings.

 Sorry for using these big words, but it makes his momma happy when he demonstrate that he did go to college. Therefore, if he uses a word you are not familiar with, feel free to substitute any of the following words according to what works best for you; thing, shit or mother-fucker.

If you are familiar with the term "catching feelings", then you will be able to understand the risk that comes with sharing intimacy. Our feelings, more accurately our emotions, create volatility within us, which by the transitive property, adds volatility to our relationships. Intimacy is where both joy and pain reside as vertical end points on an emotional continuum. I call this the Rob Base matrix. (see fig.1) Here the horizontal line represents the relationship status, with the starting point being kicking it, and the end point being in love. The vertical line represents the emotional range, with pain as the low point, and joy as the high point. The shaded area represents the range where, based on your relationship status, there is no negative emotional cost. The heart in the center represents the point where someone in the relationship is catching feelings. What I want to hip you to is what happens when you, or someone you are considering getting intimate with, begins to catch feelings.

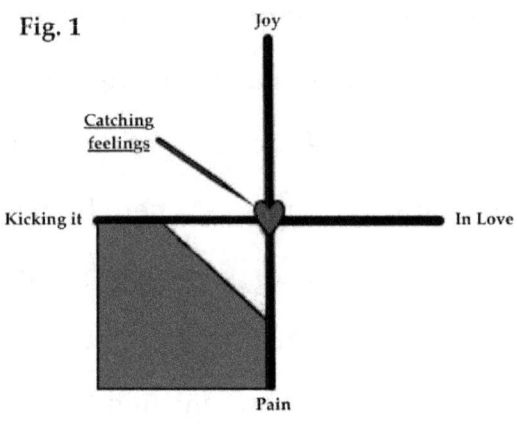

Fig. 1

As you can see from the matrix, when you are just kicking it, it's all good. As you move toward catching feelings, you also move closer toward potential pain. Once either individual catches feelings you become vulnerable to the full range of the Rob Base. It is natural for each of us to protect our feelings. I get that. In fact, some folks will go as far as blocking their joy, to guard against potential pain. Conversely, there are also people who expose themselves to a disproportionate amount of pain in respect to the joy they might receive. Most of you don't fall into either of these groups, but if you do. .

. Hopefully, you find a good professional relationship (preferably with a therapist) before you get into a personal relationship.

Most of us fall somewhere in the middle. We use a set of self-imposed constraints to deal with the perceived increase in vulnerability. These constraints come in the form of pre-requisites that are put in place in order to artificially control how quickly someone we decided to kick it with, can advance toward the in love end of the line. It's kind of like Chutes and Ladders. You do some shit right, you get to climb on up and get closer to the finish line. Fuck up one time too many, or in some cases just once, and your ass just might catch fire from how fast you're sliding down.

These constraints sometime derive from cultural/religious morals, some other type of self-imposed social beliefs, or Oprah. I'm not hating on any of these, particularly not Oprah. I may joke about the church, but only because the Pope is like an 80-year-old dude. I'm pretty sure I could whip his ass, but do you remember what the hell Oprah did to Harpo! "All's my life I's had to fight". I ain't f@#kin wit Oprah. Regardless of where they come from, these constraints all end up being the gate-keepers to the intimacy game changer; the First Use of Carnal Knowledge, commonly referred to as: get-ting busy, knocking boots, bumpin ugly, smashing, or the more technical sexual intercourse. Call it what you want, it's all still fucking, and it can change everything.

Now I would be seriously in the wrong if I did not take some time to talk about the word fuck-ing. I apologize to all who find the word offensive or vulgar, because honestly, at times, it is – depend-ing on the social setting. However, it is also a rare and beautiful word, kind of like the word aloha. I always thought the word aloha was so cool because it means both hello and good-bye. Well, the word fuck works in a similar way. You can say, "Hey let's fuck" which, for the record, is the best way you can ever say hello. While you can also say, "Hey, fuck you" which is the ultimate expression of good-bye. Additionally, the word fuck can represent the degree to which you want something or have done something that exceeds all other measurements. As an example, someone who wants something really bad, doesn't even come close to someone who wants something really fucking bad. As you can see, even though the word indicates a high degree, it can still be accentuated by a preceding adverb like really or a trailing adverb like royally, e.g. You fucked up royally!

As we look at the application of the word with respect to personal relationships, the word needs to be acknowledged as a tipping point. This simply means that at some point in the personal relationship, prior to fucking, a decision has to be made by each individual if this relationship will involve fucking or not. A key aspect for you to understand is that this is not necessarily the decision to engage in fucking at the precise moment, but only if this relationship has the potential to make it to fucking at a future time. Ok, so unless you're from West Virginia or a Mormon, familial relationships are obviously excluded from the fucking decision. No worries, there are still plenty of fish in the sea that aren't your uncle brother.

As with so many aspects of life, men and women approach the fucking decision very differently. Women are more pragmatic and calculating.

Ladies, do not get full of yourselves here. This is not to say that you are any smarter than men, you just employ a different set of skills.

Men, on the other hand, are more impulsive and untidy. Fellas, please don't feel like I'm throwing you under the bus. I know how intelligent and solution oriented, we can be...when we are thinking with the right head.

Ladies (and I use the word ladies intentionally) make their fucking decision in mere seconds upon meeting a man. Now I know this may sound impulsive, be it really is not. The reason that they are capable of making this decision so quickly is because they have spent the majority of their lives developing and codifying the pre-requisites necessary to meet their fucking criteria. In other words, women make the fucking decision based on principles. I will add that many a woman's troubles come from letting a few of those prerequisites slide with the wrong man. An important characteristic about women is that they can make their fucking decision and never act on it, or delay action until all of the pre-requisites are met and contestant number one has jumped through every goddamn hoop she dangled that pussy behind.

Men arrive at the fucking decision in the same way most people buy a Snickers bar. Not to suggest anything bad about Snickers, but no one walks into the store with the intent to buy a Snickers bar. However, if a man finds himself just standing in line, and it's right there in his face, flaunting all that sweet chocolate and sticky caramel right in his mutha-fuckin face, he's liable to get a little snacky so... like the commercial points out; "you are not yourself when you're hungry." There is no rhyme or reason to the decision. It is impetuosity in its purest form. Unfortunately, that is what can also lead to it being so messy; it's just not always well thought out. On face value, this may seem to put my brothers in arms in a bad light, but I am not judging, just explaining my point of view. If you keep reading though, I will hip you all to the reason that this is not about right or wrong, it is just about the way we are. Contrary to how women think, men make the fucking decision and attempt to act on it immediately. All men need is an opening (no pun intended).

What is important for both men and women to take away is this central truth: you get to choose who you fuck. Admittedly, this does not sound like anything profound or life changing, which is what makes the decision even easier to get wrong. Decisions are decisions – good, bad, or indifferent. As always, actions speak louder than words. The act of sex has the ability to alter the personal relationship more substantially than anything we could say. It can cause things to get all kinds of twisted. You get to choose who you fuck, but remember, not everyone can handle the potential emotional ramifications that can occur after having sex with you. Oh, and just to be perfectly clear, I am only talking about consensual fucking between two adults; Catholic priests and other rapists should burn in hell!

🕴 *I am sorry for that outburst, but the elephant was in the room. By the way, if you are keeping score, it is Kali 2 Catholics 0 and that is just in this chapter.*

You get to choose who you fuck, but understand that consensual fucking, per se, derives from one of two possible origins: Love or Lust. Love, which I characterize as a deep emotional attachment; founded or unfounded, reciprocated or unreciprocated, towards a person, place or thing, that takes time to develop. I'm not offended if you go with Webster's definition on this one, but it isn't as funny as mine.

Love is a beautiful thing, especially when it is founded and reciprocated. We feel so connected with another person emotionally, that it is only natural to connect physically with that person. On the surface, love seems like a safer option than lust, but you can believe that at your own peril. "Why?", you may ask. It's because love is rooted in emotions. This means that love can be irrational, volatile, and like the good Dr. Jekyll, it has a dark Hyde, I mean side. Acquiring equanimity – the ability to manage one's emotions – is a critical evolutionary step. It's the exact same skill required to become a Jedi, and to survive a personal relationship that involves fucking, a Jedi be you must.

Now behind curtain number two, we have love's naughty, sexier sibling, lust. Please hold your applause. Lust is fucking for fun which, to no one's surprise, puts it at the top on the Catholic hit list of seven deadly sins. This just proves that Catholics are no fucking fun. Lust is edgy and thrilling, which also makes it very risky. Lust is like theme music playing in your head while your own personal hype

man is shouting at you "yeah baby, yeah baby."
Careful though! Lust can get you jammed up. Lust
is particularly dangerous because it does not require
that there be a relationship at all, but let's save the
conversation about the Romans for another book.

*Did you catch that one? It was a little more
subtle. The whole Romans and orgy thing, with
orgies being like the quintessential example of
lust and Romans - wait for it -are Catholic. I
really don't have anything against religion,
in and of itself, or Catholicism for that matter;
but I couldn't make this shit up if I tried. The
irony is just delicious. I digress. let's move on.*

Lust can also mask itself as love, particularly if the
fucking is good. You have to keep your head. Just
because you love the dick or the pussy, doesn't
mean you're in love with the owner. This is not to
say that what began as lust cannot turn into love. It
can! However, that only occurs when you put time

into becoming more intimate with the other person. When you start sharing things beside orgasms. Remember love takes time.

So now you're fucking wit me, and nothing, I mean nothing, can take a personal relationship from just kicking it, to catching feelings faster than sex. So if your personal relationship could be characterized as any of the following: friends with benefits, dating, co-habituating, or a simple jump off. It's time to ask yourself "How did _we_ get here?" You both must have made a fucking decision that the relationship could go this far; that is how you both got here. What is a little more ambiguous is the basis for each of your respective decisions. Do you know why you made your decision? I sure as hell hope so. Now, do you know the basis for your partner's decision? Aha, see the only thing that you can determine with any certainty is lust is the threshold for a fucking relationship. Therefore, your partner would have had to reach lust at a minimum. Feeling kinda sexy aren't you? What is still unknown is if your partner has progressed to love. A key indicator in a fucking relationship is the difference between where the two parties fall on the continuum of lust to love. By our nature, (actually I'm using by our nature because it sounds more scientific and shit, it really is just my opinion) men tend to be at the low end toward lust, (shout-out to out to a Tribe Called Quest) and women on the high end toward love. There is a reason for that.

You may have noticed that I did not include marriage in my list of personal relationship options in association with the fucking decision. Well, let's be honest. Nowadays the fucking decision is made and acted on long before the marriage decision. Nonetheless, the omission was because I recognize marriage as a very different type of personal relationship. It ain't for everybody. Lust may have you catching feelings. And catching feelings may make you fall in love. And that love that the two of you share may ultimately get you into a marriage, but none of that shit is enough to keep you in a marriage. For marriage to work, you have to surpass the instincts and emotions of lust and love, and acquire something real, something more stable and sustainable – something called responsibility.

I'm just saying that marriage is a unique and complex relationship. It is such a complex topic, that even though the things I will cover in this book can apply within a marriage, marriage needs a book all to itself (hint, hint). What I will share with you, is a theory that I developed about matrimonial and pseudo-matrimonial relationships in general. I call it the Three Pillars Principle. Oh, and pseudo-matrimonial just means people who are playing house or shacking up, basically pretending like they are married without the ring or the accountability to one another. Note that I did say accountability not commitment.

Guys have been catching a bad rap for years about commitment. A man has been with his woman for six years, but Essence and Cosmopolitan say he can't commit. Ladies your man commits to you long before he asks you to marry him, if he's a good man.

The Three Pillars are what I have determined to be the deoxyribonucleic acid of matrimonial relationships.

♼ Yeah, I know he could have just said DNA, but then his mother wouldn't be getting her money's worth now would she? If you aren't sure of the analogy, DNA is the building blocks of life, so the Three Pillars are the building blocks for a marriage.

Now the foundation for a marriage must be built on love. Trying to build the foundation from lust, or any of the other seven deadly sins will only lead to doom. Even building it on love (as Tina Turner so poignantly sang) may not be enough to keep it from falling apart, unless you build upon that foundation of love with an understanding of the Three Pillars Principle.

The first thing I need you to recognize is that there are three pillars, not two, and not four. This means that a relationship is uneven. It's odd, so structurally it is already not in your favor. This doesn't mean it can't work, just that it requires you – wait for it – pay attention to shit in order to maintain the balance. Furthermore, you must understand the universal truth of Luther Vandross. A room is still a room, but a house is not a home, unless you learn to balance the three pillars. If one of those pillars is damaged, the home may not be as balanced, but it may still be able to stand. However, if you let two pillars get damaged, the whole thing will collapse in short order, possibly causing irreparable damage to people (namely you) and property (meaning half yo shit).

The first pillar is Communication. Information has to be effectively exchanged between two people. This isn't just about talking and listening; this is about sending messages and ensuring that the messages are received, interpreted, and understood as they were intended. Communication is a two – way street, therefore the other side is equally as important. It is necessary to confirm that the information being received is, in fact, the information that the sender intended. This is a lot harder than you think, so read it again to make sure you understand me.

The second pillar is Finances. If you endeavor to be in a marriage, always be mindful that there ain't nuthin going on but the rent! There is no honey if your money is funny. Nothing makes a marriage come crashing down like the threat of foreclosure. All jokes aside, it's nice when you are making money, but it's more important that someone in the relationship knows how to manage it, particularly the money you spend that you don't actually have. Credit cards are the work of the devil. Many relationships have ended due to irreconcilable Visa accounts.

Finally, the third pillar is Fucking. You had to know I was coming back to it. Even when you care about someone, time has a way to erode those emotions of attachment and attraction. Sex is an important technique to be able to reconnect and reestablish the feelings that you have for one another. The activity forces closeness and vulnerability, which contribute to strengthening trust. And if you both can handle your business, it provides physical pleasure and relieves stress. Lack of sex or ineffective sex is almost always as close to a deal breaker as you can get. A healthy and satisfying sex life is essential to the sustainability of a marriage. Without it a couple will begin to drift apart.

I could go on and on about marriage and my three pillars, but it would probably be like writing a second book, (wink). The important thing to take away about all personal relationships is this; you should probably write this down. Personal relationships are all intimate. Intimacy is synonymous with vulnerability; therefore, as the intimacy grows toward catching feelings, our level of vulnerability grows as well. Catching feelings expand our opportunity for higher levels of both joy and pain, so be careful, particularly when it comes to making a decision about having sex, since that is the fastest way to catch feelings. Be sure you know whether you're on the high end or just creeping lustfully on the low end. I'm not saying one side is any better than the other is. You just need to recognize everything in this relationship changes now that you're fuckin wit me.

PART II

THE NATURE OF THINGS

CHAPTER THREE

This Chick Is Crazy!

Take One

Earlier, I mentioned that women were more likely than men to be at the high end; more specifically the love end, of the lust/love continuum. The explanation for this is easy; it's because women are crazy! Please don't take that the wrong way. I mean it with the utmost respect, not to belittle or deride. I am just submitting it for your consideration. The truth is that women and men really are not that different. In fact, the difference is merely one Y chromosome; men have it, and women don't.

This Y chromosome is like a get out of jail-free card, emancipating the male human from the experience of menstruation and pregnancy, which, from my male perspective, is a sweet deal. Nonetheless, I have to admit that the greatest human ability is to give birth to new life, which only a woman can do. Ladies, you are amazing. I am not trying to kiss up to you here. You're still crazy, amazingly crazy. Since we have introduced the topic of babies, let me put this out for you to nibble on. Always be mindful that this ability is a blessing not a parlor trick. It most certainly is not something you should leave to chance, because the true miracle is if you can raise your babies to be decent people, which is more likely to happen if you are a good person yourself and prepared emotionally, intellectually, and financially for the responsibility of raising a child. Like big momma would say, the last thing we need is ignorant ass people filling the world up with ignorant ass babies. Check Netflix for "Idiocracy."

Unfortunately for you ladies, God works in mysterious ways. So along with this awesome ability comes what I like to refer to as the cuckoo clock. This cuckoo clock, fueled by the hormone estrogen, can get women all wound up; and like the clock it is named for, it is only a matter of time before a woman gets a little cuckoo for coco puffs. This is no fault of the woman per se; some chicks are straight whack jobs regardless of estrogen.

🕴 *And that's why you need to save up a few vacation days at the job, just in case that chick snaps.*

It is just the way that the chromosomes and the hormone decks have been stacked for her. Think about this for a second. Say there was an intergalactic visitor from a completely different planet far across the galaxy. The alien arrives at the planet Earth. It has some idea of what human beings are based on TubeYou (it's like YouTube, but for aliens), but would like to ask you some questions. The conversation might go a little like this.

Alien - "How does the female function"?

Mr. Q – Hmm, well it's somewhat complicated. A woman is sort of designed to run off an internal clock of procreation. So about every 28 days, she completes a cycle.

Alien – Cycle?

Mr. Q – Yeah, it's kind of nature's way of keeping everyone on their toes.

Alien – Is it violent or dangerous?

Mr. Q – That depends on your definition of violence, but I can tell you there will more than likely be some yelling, there is a lot of blood involved, and it may require someone to need emergency medical attention.

Alien – Oh, you mean when she is giving birth to one of your young and having to push a 7lb miniature human out of a 3 inch wide opening.

Mr. Q – No, I mean if your ass is dumb enough to say something stupid when she's on her period.

Alien – Oh my, and what about you. Do male humans also have a clock?

Mr. Q - Yes, time to eat, time to sleep, time to fuck, and not always in that order.

Alien – So the female human gets 28 days to attempt impregnation, which results in a 9 month gestation that requires the occupation of her womb by a miniature human.

Mr. Q – Yup!

Alien – And if she fails to be impregnated, she becomes hormonally imbalanced and bleeds profusely from her womb for 5-7 days.

Mr. Q – You got it.

Alien – But won't the loss of blood lead to her death?

Mr. Q – Nah, but it can get a little messy, so to keep the flow under control she plugs herself up with an evil tethered sponge. Shit's crazy right?

Alien – Indeed, shit is, as you human's say, cra cra for the reals tho.

It is a crazy cycle, and here is why I say that it makes women crazy. Thanks to estrogen, women are hormonally (not sure if that is a word but fuck it, it sounds good) designed to be nurturers. Since you ladies have the babies, you need to be sensitive to others, caring, and supportive. All the things men suck at or don't care about. However, this generally is the reason that women tend to be driven more by emotions than their male counterparts, who for the most part, find it hard to be caring and supportive of anything beyond their stomach and their penis; but I will get to that later. Emotions are a powerful and highly flammable fuel, so much so, that they are very difficult to sustain. Let me give you an example from my childhood.

I am the youngest of four boys, with four years between my closest sibling and me. It really doesn't seem like a huge disparity now that we are grown, but when you are 8 going up against 12 and 13 yr. olds, it's a huge mismatch if your name isn't Shaquille. My brothers would wait until my parents were going out to beat me down for all the tattle telling I did. Yes, I was a snitch. Snitches may get stitches, but I was not taking any ass whuppins from my dad for the team. My brothers would always wait about 15 minutes after my parents left to make sure they weren't pulling the old once around the block catch you in the act move. Then they would proceed to pummel me, and I would just cry and cry. Somehow my knucklehead brothers understood that crying is a release of very powerful emotions; therefore, it is extremely hard to sustain. Eventually, you get exhausted and pass the fuck out. By the time my parents got back home, I was sleeping like a baby and they were none the wiser.

When you are more emotional, as women generally are in comparison to men, the emotions are not only hard to sustain, but just as difficult to restrain. Holla if you hear me fellas. So the stage is set on day 1 of a 28 day crazy cycle. Now fellas you need to pay attention to this shit, so read this part twice if necessary. Each day of the cycle brings a woman one day closer in preparation to be pregnant. This means that each day of the cycle, a woman may be different emotionally than she was the day before. To be more specific, she gets a little crazier each day until the cycle resets. It's very subtle, and very easy to miss in the beginning. I know there are some women reading this who are saying, I don't know what I'm talking about. However, before you are so quick to hate on me, maybe you should check which day of your cycle you are on right now, because next week your crazy ass might think what I'm saying makes me a genius.

As each day passes, the hormones are increasing, raging, and it is completely out of a woman's control. The estrogen is messing with her emotions, but it's not just that. Her body is physically changing as well. That's right! She is ovulating (Google it, cause I don't have time) which makes her skin clear up, and her breasts enlarge so she is more attractive. Oh, and her appetite is greater than that family of fat asses you see when you eat at the Chinese buffet, only not for food. She is hungry for sex. Ladies if you can give me a minute, I am going to take a moment here to speak directly to my male readers right now. Men, if you don't know what ovulation is, it's because you ain't fucking listening. I told your ass to Google it four sentences ago. So Google it, print it out and put it in a frame. Why? Because more than likely it was ovulation, not your smooth talk, or your funky ass cologne, or your

Groupon deal for two at Red Lobster that got you laid. It was ovulation, and ovulation is truly man's best friend. All you had to do was not say or do anything stupid for two hours, and she was going to fuck you. Ladies, you can join back in. Now where was I? Oh right, the crazy cycle. So now she is ovulating, which is essentially being in heat. Remember a woman's body wants to get pregnant, which requires precise timing and a large donation of sperm; and frankly, hormones are not too particular about who the donations come from. No pun intended.

This is the stage of the cycle where the hormones of the women completely align with the hormonal directives of men and therefore, the time when the relationship is at its best for both parties. Unfortunately, time waits for no one, and soon the blissful days of ovulation, copulation, and fornication give way to the dreadful emotional holocaust of pre-menstrual syndrome or PMS.

How fucking awful does something have to be, to be classified as a syndrome anyway? I want to be clear, PMS is not always this horrific thing, but can you really blame her if it is. I mean honestly, (insert book title here). No, fellas we can't, nor do we have the right to be surprised when it hits. Like my daddy told me, anyone that gets hit by a train deserved it, it's not like the muthafucker snuck up on you. I'm sure there is a nice clinical explanation for why PMS has the effect on the female emotional state that it does. I probably could have done some research here and provided you with an academically impressive synopsis of it all, but why should I go full Britannica when you are so willing to accept Wikipedia? Therefore, I'll just keep telling you what I think. Ladies your body wants to get pregnant. Apparently, God wants you to get pregnant too. It's the whole be fruitful and multiply thing. Once the body realizes that you screwed it over by not getting knocked up, the body has all the hormones flowing at full capacity with no baby to nurture. Surely there will be hell to pay, and hell hath no fury like a hormone scorned. Therefore, it unleashes its stockpiles of estrogen upon a woman, most certainly in an attempt to cause irreparable damage to her relationship with the person who conspired to avoid pregnancy. So for the better part of a week the hormones lay siege to the woman's relationship by heightening emotions to a level where calling her bipolar could be an understatement. And then she gets a visit from Mother Nature.

As if she doesn't already have enough shit to deal with because of that bitch at work (nobody likes you Jessica!), her dumb-ass man, and spoiled little midgets she calls kids, now she has to bleed for the next five days or so. Inserting, lining, checking, removing, replacing, leaking, spotting, heavy flow, light days and who is this bitch in the commercial riding horseback? Are you fucking kidding me? Ladies I applaud you, 'cause I sure as he'll couldn't do it. Only a crazy person could.

So what does this all mean? Women are going to continue through this cycle month after month. Year after year, until menopause kicks in. Then all the crazy gets really crazy as hormones are determined to go out in an epic blaze of glory. I'm talking scorched earth. What do you think causes those hot flashes? It's the hormones setting her ass on fire. However, if the woman can just make it to the other side, there is a calm that awaits her. Think of the women you know that have gone through the change. They don't give a fuck about anything anymore. You can kiss her ass, her man can kiss her ass, them kids can kiss her ass, that damn job can kiss her ass, and the ass kissing list just keeps going. We have to accept that women's nature leans emotional. Combine this with a cycle that exacerbates the already fluid emotions, and now add the shit that a person has to deal with in a normal day. Why would anyone fault you for being crazy? So embrace it ladies. Own it! Once you do, maybe, just maybe you can keep it from fucking up your relationships; and I say that with utmost sincerity.

Take Two

Earlier, I made the statement that acquiring the ability to manage one's emotions is a critical evolutionary step. Therefore, now is as good a time as any to have a little more substantive conversation about why I hold that statement to be true. If you can follow this logic string, then you can follow

where I am coming from. Not trying to be bragga-
docious,

🕴 *ooo isn't that a good word. See what*
can happen if you send your kids to col-
lege.

but now may be a good time to take a few notes.
Contrary to the saying, actions do not speak louder
than words. In fact, actions without words are in-
explicable, almost invariably leaving one to ask the
question…wtf? The annoying thing about having to
explain our action is the universal expectation to
pass the Earth, Wind, and Fire test. . . also known as
Reasons. People expect that we have a reason for
what we do, and not just any reason, a good reason,
a reasonable reason.

Emotions are impulsive, impetuous little
creatures, so they have very little time or need for a
reason. Besides, reason requires thinking, and we all

know emotional reactions are borne in the passion at the moment, right? Well, generally yes. However, crazy works differently, and this is why it is so important for women to embrace their crazy. Crazy doesn't know it is crazy. Crazy thinks it is completely fine, and the real crazy ones are the people who think crazy is crazy. Did you follow that? Shit's crazy right? However, it is true. I'll show you. Ladies have you ever called your man (and he may not even be your man, but your crazy ass ain't trying to hear that), and he doesn't answer his phone. What do you think? Here's another scenario. Ladies, let's say you are with your man and his phone rings, and he doesn't answer it. What do you think now?

Well, a reasonable person would think in the first scenario that the man was busy and not available to speak at the time and leave it at that. Not a crazy person. A crazy person will think "what the fuck is he doing that he can't answer the god damn phone," and immediately call back. If he doesn't answer the phone this time, crazy will do one of three things: 1) call again, 2) call his momma, or 3) drive to his house or job and set shit off. Now a reasonable person would think in the second scenario, he isn't answering his phone because he either doesn't want to be rude, or he doesn't want to talk with the person calling, and leave it at that. Not a crazy person, a crazy person will think "that's probably some bitch calling" and immediately ask, "Who was that?" Now in his mind, he's thinking, bitch it's my phone; it obviously wasn't for you. However, he will only let that thought come out of his mouth, if he's crazy too.

Far too many relationships are jeopardized on a daily basis because of the inability of women to recognize that they are crazy at the time when things are getting heated. Knowledge is power, so it is critically important for a woman to be in tune with her cycle, so she knows when to stop trusting her own judgement and emotional impulses.

The next thing women need to do is give the people she cares most about a heads up. Stop pretending that you aren't getting crazy and start preparing people for when the shit is about to pop off. Put that shit on the family calendar. I'm just saying, if you don't take the time to prepare for the impending storm, then you are forced to rely on a George Bush led FEMA to help rescue your relationship from the devastation caused by hurricane Halle Berry. Halle baby, at some point you have to know it's you, right? Anyway ladies, what we have here is a failure to communicate. There need to be forecasts, Doppler radar tracking, category levels of the potential force, clear instructions on where to get essential re-sources, and where to seek shelter.

Now there will be some people reading this who think I am intentionally exaggerating the metaphor to be provocative. Fuck you! You can take this shit lightly, but you do so at your own peril. Real talk though, sometimes it is better to pack up the kids and spend a few days at your momma's house, than try to weather some unpredictable crazy shit. This is particularly the case if you and your partner have the tendency to throw gas on fires and escalate the madness. Fuck around and say something that you can never take back or do something that leaves you with a charge. It's not worth it, especially when just accepting that you are crazy, can avoid it all.

I'm not naive enough to believe that any one of us can always control our emotions. As I have stated, emotions are volatile. However, if you have been paying attention to shit, what I'm telling you is that the emotions and the crazy have to be managed, which is not the same as being controlled. I also want everyone to understand that this isn't just on the ladies. In relationships, both people have a role to play. So, to my fellas out there, you need to know when to leave her the fuck alone. Stop running your mouth when you know she is on the edge. Stop doing dumb shit in the midst of the storm. If you think I'm bull-shitting you, watch just one episode of Snapped. If you love each other, then you need to work together on this to get to the other side, otherwise... WTFDYE.

CHAPTER FOUR

Fuck Him!

Take One

This is probably going to be one of the more difficult subjects in the book for me to discuss. Oddly enough, it is complicated for two diametrically opposed reasons. On the one side, this is a difficult area to cover because of the unwritten man code. Some of the women reading this may be wondering what the "man code" is. Well, "man code" is simply the things that every man knows. However, he doesn't talk about it in the company of women. It's kind of like Fight Club, and I'm already in violation by admitting that the code actually exists. Therefore, I run the serious risk of being ostracized from the brotherhood of men simply by sharing these things with you. So I hope you ladies appreciate it, and I hope the men out there recognize that I'm doing this for the greater good.

On the other side of my conundrum is the struggle I have as a father of a young girl, who will grow to be an amazing woman, to whom I am obligated to equip with the information she will need to navigate the potentially turbulent waters of relationships with men. That is of course if men are her preference.

🕴 *I have to put the disclaimer in because I love her unconditionally, and I really don't want to be bothered with the LGBT community screaming homophobe. That's not to suggest that gay people are more likely to scream than any other group, it was simply a figure of speech. Unless of course it involves Diana Ross or Cher, then they are definitely more likely to scream. And while I'm at it, how did bisexuals get into that group? I mean they are kind of part timers so do they get full benefits or... oh never mind.*

What I was trying to say is that I have to write this chapter for my daughter. Otherwise, I could be leaving her to rely on the misguided philosophies of some pseudo-psychological article published in a Cosmopolitan or Essence magazine. You know the articles, the ones you see promoted on the covers of the magazines in the checkout aisle of the grocery store. These teaser stories crack me up: *What men want, What men don't want, Why men stay, Why men leave* and of course the chart topping *Why Men Cheat.*

Some intellectual with two or three letters after their name wants to lead you to believe they have figured it all out for you. Just for the record, they haven't figured out a damn thing. There's no money in giving you answers, so they give you just enough to keep you subscribing.

I guess the real story should be *Why Women are Addicted to Articles about what men want, don't want, stay, don't stay, and of course cheat.* Women like to say they read these articles because they are just looking for "A Few Good Men", but that isn't the truth; and as the movie so famously stated ladies, you can't handle the truth. Nonetheless, I'm going to tell it to you. I'll cover why women are so interested in those articles in the next chapter. For now, I want to address a few things about men. So to my women readers, you have my daughter to thank for what I am about to hip you to. As for my male readers, just think of what I write as some of the shit you wish you could say to your woman, but are afraid to try, because as we discussed earlier, that chick is crazy!

It would only stand to reason that if a woman's behavior is attributable to the effects of hormones, then the same would hold true for men. Well, if that is what you were thinking, then you are right. I'm so proud of you. What you may not realize though, is that the male hormone testosterone is one of the most dangerous substances on the planet. Ok that's a bit of hyperbole. It's not like plutonium or anything, but it is some powerful stuff. Power being the operative word. Testosterone and estrogen are produced by both men and women, just in different proportions. Below I have put together a completely unscientific comparison of the two hormones, and their effects. Before anyone starts blasting me on Twitter (@kalistrikesback), as if this disclaimer is going to stop that, this chart is a generalization to make a point. Well, actually to make my point, but since I'm the guy writing the book, and you're the one reading it, I'm cool with the way that works out.

On the far left are general factors for both men and women. The next two columns give the effect of estrogen and testosterone, respectively, on those factors.

	ESTROGEN	TESTOSTERONE
BASIC INSTINCT	nurturing	aggression
BODY IMAGE	adds fat to attract males	burns fat to attract females
REPRODUCTION	menstruation	ejaculation
RELATIONSHIP DRIVER	love	lust
IMPACTS SEX DRIVE	no	yes

So from this chart we can surmise that women are softer more supple creatures, driven less by sex, more by love, with the desire to create life and nurture it. Men on the other hand, are muscled creatures (if you're lucky, right ladies?) driven by lust to aggressively pursue sex in order to ejaculate on everything. Again, not the most scientific answer, but still pretty damn accurate. I won't go as far as calling men fucking machines, because we all know that every man can have sex, but they all can't fuck. However, I will say men are biologically engineered and chemically fueled by testosterone to pursue sex. God said be fruitful and multiply, but like any smart parent, he knows kids don't listen. So he designed it that when a male hits puberty his testosterone levels increase tenfold to drive the desire. He made the sensation of an orgasm as intoxicating as any drug, and equally addictive.

Fellas, don't make the mistake of taking this as a license to act a fool. It's not. If you are in a personal relationship with someone, particularly a fucking relationship, you're responsible for protecting that person from your hormones. Just like the ladies need to own their crazy, men need to own their horny. Owning it is the best way not to let someone exploit it against you. You need to put it out there so it becomes a known part of the equation, rather than some unspoken awkward tension. Just as a disclaimer before the lawyers come knocking on my door because your dumbass can't comprehend nuance, I am not suggesting that you go all full disclosure of every freak nasty shit that runs through your perverted mind. Please, don't do that! However, it is fair to both parties if you acknowledge that it is real, and like the crazy – it needs to be effectively managed.

Take Two

A few years back, there was a really good book by Steven Levitt and Stephen Dubner called "Freakonomics: a Rogue Economist Explores the Hidden Side of Everything." The book is an eye-opening read, laying out the correlation between economics and social behaviors in ways we may have never considered before. Reading the book provided me with one of those aha moments of clarity about the man/woman social construct. I introduce this concept to you to explain the answer to a question that is asked repeatedly, but never answered truthfully... Why Do Men Cheat?

That's right, the answer to why do men cheat, is freakonomics. It comes down to the basic principles of supply and demand. A man's demand for sex is second only to his demand for food. Have you ever thought about how much a man eats? Three meals a day plus snacks, seven days a week. That's a minimum of 21 meals a week. So if we were to assume that sex is half as much in demand as food, (and trust me, it is a lot more than half) that would be 10 times a week a man is hungry to get his freak on. Unfortunately for my brothers, we can't stock our pantry and refrigerator with orgasms that we can pop in the microwave when the urge strikes us. Trust me, if pussy and blowjobs were things a man could stock up in the freezer, they would be the best selling hot pockets in history. Unfortunately, it doesn't work that way. "Sex Packets" is still just a song. If a man wants to get his cum on, he has to be prepared to negotiate with his woman because his dick isn't going to suck itself, and she controls 100% of supply and access to The Pussy.

Yes, I did just refer to it as The Pussy. Anything as influential as "The Pussy" deserves its proper respect. Trust me; it wasn't Helen's face that launched those thousand ships.

🕴 *If you don't get that reference, please put this book down now and google "the face that launched a thousand ships". Go ahead, I can wait. Ok, I have to put in a little public service announcement here. I really appreciate you reading this book, but if you had to look up that reference; please, please, please make sure your kids read that other book. Nothing I say will help them get into college, and a mind is a terrible thing to waste. Thank you.*

My point about The Pussy is this: there has never been, nor will there ever be a war fought over some dick. I know there are a lot of reality shows like the whole housewives' franchise that make it seem otherwise, but the reality is those are just some ignorant ass chicks playing up to a camera, fighting over the money that is sponsoring the dick of some trifflin' fool. It ain't the same.

When the amount of orgasms being supplied to a man falls well short of his demand, he seeks to source his needs from other available methods or suppliers to the market, simple supply and demand. How do you think the porn industry has become a 4 billion dollar a year industry? Trust me, is not because of the acting or the intriguing plots. In fact, I don't think anyone has ever actually seen the end of a porno. I know I haven't. Strip clubs never go out of business due to a lack of customers, and if someone tells you that the food at Hooters is good, it's only because it comes with a side of tits and a good visual for him to jack his dick later.

I know there are some women out there that don't like their men watching porn. You think to yourself that he only watches that because you are not enough, and he wants the kind of things and women in those movies. And I say movies, because

I hope there aren't men out there still using magazines. Hello, the Internet! Anyway, ladies you're mostly wrong, most men completely understand that porn is not real, but just like fake tits, we don't care that it's not real. (Just like everyone knows reality tv isn't real; it's manufactured drama from untrained wannabe actors). Furthermore, ladies it isn't that you aren't enough; for most men, you are everything they want in their reality. However, porn isn't about any reality; it's just about visual stimulation to allow a man to take matters into his own hands.

Masturbation is the staple of a man's orgasm diet; it's kind of like rice. It goes with everything. If a man is feeling nervous, jack off. If he's feeling angry, jack off. Need to perk up, jack off. Need to calm down, jack off. Need to start the day, why not a little jerk. Want a good night sleep, just rub one out. Feeling a little horny, but your lady isn't home, beat your dick like it just scuffed your new Jordan's. Yeah, masturbation is a staple. It's inexpensive, unless you're into high end lubricants (which I do recommend). Although it is not a full meal, it can hold a man over through the lean times, which in some cases can occur every few hours or so. However, masturbation isn't anything that he will ever get full off of. Eventually he will want something a little more substantial.

Some men turn to the world's oldest profession, prostitution. This is why I don't like Kobe Bryant. When Kobe got himself all Chubb Rock in Colorado.

If you're wondering what Chubb Rock means, it refers to his song Caught Up from back in the 80s. If you are a little younger, you can substitute Usher.

Kobe made the statement that maybe he should have used prostitutes like one of his teammates, except he actually named the teammate, who was married. Here is my problem with what Kobe did. No one likes a dumb ass trying to be a smart ass. It doesn't work. Therefore, when his dumb ass made the decision to fuck around with the skank white girl, it led to the rape charge. Then he wants to be a smart ass by making that comment; but the irony is, if he wasn't a dumb ass, he would have used a prostitute, paid for her services and never been put on blast. I'm not advocating the use of prostitutes as the right thing to do, but in Kobe's case, it at least would have been smart. I won't even get into the whole punk ass throwing another brother under the bus shit. Ok, deep breath. Wow, prostitution the world's oldest profession? Not doctors, not lawyers, not accountants, but women telling men what they want to hear, pretending like they are interested, and making him cum any way his money can pay for – supply and demand. The tools of their trade have proven so effective that they have made their way into mainstream culture. How many of you ladies own platform stiletto heels, g-strings, garter belts, thigh-high stockings, bustiers, lipstick, and false eyelashes? These items used to be in the brothels and street corners, then the clubs and bars, now it's just Tuesday at the office. Well, if you think you look good in it, then thank prostitution for blazing the trail so you can get a free drink at the bar. However, just don't be offended when the guy buying that drink asks you how much for a hand job.

Then there are the men who rely on the free market to supply their demand. Obviously, this is overt if the man himself is also on the free market. However, there are many a person, man and woman alike, that are not on the free market, but they still are shopping unbeknownst to their significant other. These people are considered cheaters; or more biblically accurate, adulterer's. Ooooooooo. It could be a jump off, a hook up, an NSA (no strings attached) FWB (friend with benefits), or on the DL.

I have to say, I am pretty disturbed by the appropriation of the term, down low. There was a time when down low just meant that; information, or for our purpose relationships, were kept undercover, on the hush, you know to protect the innoce...well guilty. Nonetheless, on the down low now is myopically branded to a particularly type of undercover relationship. What can you do?

Men and women have sex outside of their public facing relationships for very different reasons...generally. However, sometimes they do it for the exact same reasons, but I find that women having the same reason as men is more the exception than the rule. You should be getting a little better at paying attention by now, so you should have noticed that I used the phrase "sex outside their... relationship." I say this instead of cheating as to not pass judgement or take sides. The term cheater and adulterer are strong and potentially hurtful words, that usually gives no examination into the possible reasons behind the actions or if there is any malicious intent. Now some of you are reacting to this by sucking your damn teeth because you feel like it doesn't matter. That's cool; you still get to call it whatever you want honey.

I promised you an answer to the question why men cheat. I gave it to you. I know you probably were hoping for some more sophisticated explanation of this morally bankrupt act, this heinous violation of trust. Sorry, it just comes down to supply and demand. So, what should women do? How should smart women adapt to this irrefutable realization? I say fuck him, and fuck him often!

CHAPTER FIVE

Do U Lie?

They say that there is truth in jest. This is what makes some of the greatest comedians so gut-achingly funny. One of my favorites is Chris Rock's comments about women. He so accurately informed us that women only need three things to survive; food, water and compliments. Now I know most people wouldn't consider Chris Rock on the level of

Plato, but he really is. In fact, many comedians are just modern-day philosophers. (Except for you Bliss, #blissisignorant). That's why most bits start with "did you ever wonder" or "did you ever notice", which is particularly dear to me. That's because taking notice, well paying attention, is the entire premise throughout this book.

Another Rockism has settled the debate on who are bigger liars, women, or men. Again, he gave us tremendous insight that men lie most often, but women tell the biggest lies. I have expounded on Rock's theory and put forward that the nature of the lie is as different as the nature of men and women. Men lie about their actions: what they won, who they met, and where they were last night when you couldn't reach them. Women lie about themselves: what they look like, what they think like, and what the fuck they actually want.

Men tell what my momma calls outright boldface lies. This is the lie of speaking words from your mouth that your ass knows ain't true. They may be big. They may be small, but they are definitely not true. Women tell the lie of omission or secrets. It's not about the words that come out of their mouths; it's about the words they never speak. You know what Victoria's Secret is? She's a freak with an underwear fetish that gets her moist all day at work thinking about getting dicked down by Dexter St. Jacque, but shhhh you didn't hear it from me, and you won't hear it from her because women all keep secrets.

This is not to say that women don't tell lies about their actions like men do or that men don't tell lies about themselves like women. In fact, with gender boundaries becoming more blurred due to our unavoidable evolution, men and women each take on more characteristics of the other little by little. Men don't have a monopoly on lying to cover their tracks because women increasingly have tracks that need to be covered. Accordingly, women don't have exclusive rights to lying about who they are or what they want.

In relationships, more specifically professional and personal relationships, secrets can be dangerous things. If people on the job are keeping secrets from you, it probably lands you in HR or unemployment. Men aren't really good at keeping secrets, which is often the reason that they have to tell lies. We try our best to keep secrets, but we aren't as good at concealing the evidence as women.

Oooo that may come off as a taking a shot at you ladies, but I assure you it is not. Men like to brag and boast about their triumphs. It's hard to keep things under wraps with that character flaw. Ladies, and I do mean ladies, are more demure (fellas you can look up demure when you finish the chapter, it's not that long) about their activities and intentions, so discretion comes more naturally. Did you brothers see how I cleaned that up? Just remember to be cautious ladies and gentlemen. Secrets can be dangerous because they can lead to unanticipated revelations. Better known as a "surprise for yo ass" and it's not a new car. One of the casualties of becoming an adult is surprises are not as much fun. When you're a kid, they are awesome. However, when you are grown and have shit to take care of, you become a little more concerned that what is behind curtain number 2 just might be your past, ticking like a time bomb that is about to blow your shit up. It's like when his big surprise, is that he knows your "little" secret. KA-Boom!

The truth is that we all tell lies (you gotta love the irony of that line) whether the lies come directly out of our mouths or through secrets and omissions. Believe it or not, in some part, telling lies serve its purpose to keep things moving toward the greater good. Ladies, we both know you don't really like his momma. However, sometimes you have to tell a lie just to avoid bigger problems about shit that just isn't that important. Guys, if your woman asks you did you like that blowjob, what are you going to say? That it was kind of dry and toothy, not if you ever want her to give it another try...on your dick and not someone else's.

Now please don't think that I am attempting to downplay that lying is a bad thing. I'm not, but I am also not universally going to declare it as the root of all evil. I just recognize in some situations not telling the lie does more damage. So yes there is a Santa Claus, the Tooth Fairy is real, size doesn't matter, and I do think you are a good cook, why would I lie?

NOTE: I acknowledge that there are many instances where lies/secrets & omissions are far more serious and threaten our ability to maintain a relationship. That's a heavier subject than this book, but it is coming soon.

PART III

PRODUCT OF YOUR

ENVIRONMENT

CHAPTER SIX

Social Lies

A few years back there was a very popular relationship book called "Women are from Venus, Men are from Mars". It was a cute intra-galactic metaphor on the differences between men and women being as great as people from different planets. I mentioned earlier that men and women aren't really that different, aside from a chromosome here or there, so in my opinion that book is full of shit; you made a much better purchase buying this book. We definitely are not from different planets. We are simply socialized in two very distinct ways that send us down distinct paths that lead to behaviors, which in the grand scheme are meant to make us complimentary. Nonetheless these behaviors still cause men and women to struggle to understand each other.

Now there may be someone out there reading this and saying "whatchu mean sosho, sosho, sosholized" Well socialized means the impact that society or, you know what, fuck it. If you don't know, kill yourself.

 ****DISCLAIMER: THE PUBLISHERS OF THIS BOOK IN NO WAY MEAN TO SUGGEST, INTIMATE, OR IMPLY THAT ANYONE SHOULD KILL OR

HARM THEMSELVES IN ANY WAY DUE TO A LACK
OF UNDERSTANDING OF THE TERM SOCIALIZED.

Okay, Okay, the lawyers are telling me that I can't tell you to kill yourself, so please don't kill yourself, I'll explain it. Socialization is the impact, or effect, that society or culture has on the beliefs and behaviors of the individuals who make up that society. My point is this: men and women are socialized to fall into roles that impact interactions within our relationships, not just the relationships that we are in, but also the ones we pursue. All jokes aside, socialization is a tool that serves as a form of control over the norms of individuals within the society. Now you might think I'm talking about laws, which is a reasonable comparison, but socialization works differently than laws. Laws, usually, are established through some form of a governmental process. Socialization is much more gangsta. It's the unwritten rules that those in power impose on those who are not in power. If it helps, think of any social issue that is being publicly debated. On one side, you will have the established socialization of the powers that be, and on the other side you will have the blasphemy of the heretics who dare challenge being assimilated. This usually results in the haves attempting to pass actual laws to restrict the liberty of the have nots; from where you can sit on a bus, to your right to choose having a baby, to who you can or cannot marry.

So you say, "Ok Andre'. Enough with the soapbox. What does any of this have to do with relationships?" The answer, of course, is a lot. The socialization of men and women is overt yet subtle. Therefore, it is rarely challenged. In fact, it's quite the opposite. It's more often reinforced from each generation to the next. Please don't misunderstand me. I'm not saying anything is wrong with this socialization, (well technically, I'm not right now, but I will be in a moment), but we have to pay attention to its effects on us as individuals and what we bring to our relationships.

I hope I have explained this in a way that allows you to get it, if not, kil...on second thought, think of it like this. All of our relationships involve people (hopefully) and every person out there is a culmination of their heredity and environment. Now there is plenty of debate about which has more impact. Hell, Mortimer and Randolph Duke bet a dollar over this very question in the movie "Trading Places." It's the nature vs. nurture debate. However, what isn't up for debate is that both play a role regardless of which one has dominance. Therefore, we have to understand that the people in our relationships act, or more accurately react, in certain ways because they were taught to behave that way. Some behaviors are bad habits learned from parents with bad habits, bad parents, or some other influential figures in our lives. Hence the saying "the apple doesn't fall far from the tree." Personally, I prefer my own saying "the cuckoo doesn't fly far from the clock." Other behaviors and personality traits are projected on us by society and reinforced by society in order to perpetuate the traits for generations.

Good thing I'm not one of those "angry black men" who would exploit this opening to go on a completely unrelated rant on the covert implementation of a systematic plan utilizing socialization to perpetuate a slave mentality among the black Americans in a post slavery economy that has led to generations of poverty, drug abuse, broken families and incarceration. Yeah, good thing I'm not that guy right?

So let's stay on the topic. How are we social-izing our women? How are we socializing our men? And what do we need to know about one an-other in order to interact more effectively? Well, I'm glad you asked.

CHAPTER SEVEN

Women Aren't From Venus,

They're Just Insecure.

Beauty is a Beast

I hope that I still have some women reading this book after calling you all crazy. Sincerely, I mean no harm. It's just that some shit has to be put on the table so we can stop wasting time pretending like the crazy isn't real, or that there is something wrong with it, or it makes you the problem. That's not the case.

I can understand if some women are a little upset. If you are, then all I can say is what is coming next will really piss you off. Nothing like a good omelette I always say (if that reference went over your head, try jumping).

Women are socialized to be insecure, and this inherent insecurity plays a major part on the relationships they have and pursue. This socialization of women starts from the moment the sonogram determines that it's a girl. A whirlwind of decisions and accommodations are made to welcome the little "princess" into the world. Color schemes, clothes, toys, furniture, and emotional catchphrases like "daddy's little girl" (never heard daddy's little boy, have you?) are all applied to make sure this innocent child understands, without a doubt, that she is a girl. As if a vagina wasn't a strong enough statement. Of course it's not, because the vagina is about sex not gender. Everyone knows it's not the pussy that makes the woman; it's whether the shoes match the purse.

I blame Barbie. That's right, Barbie! I never liked that heifer or her dick-less boyfriend Ken. You can think I'm joking, but I'm not. I'm very serious. What exactly do these dolls teach our little girls? It's a rhetorical question. The answer is insecurity. Before I get all into the Barbie Complex, let me take a second or two to talk about baby dolls. Why the fuck do we give little girls fake babies, like having a baby is child's play. Look, I have an eight-year-old, and the last thing I want is for her to play mommy to little baby poops-a-lot—particularly at a stage in her development where she is the most impressionable. Hey honey, why don't we make pretend you're a single mom raising a child all by yourself without any financial or emotional resources to help you support another life. Yeah, let's start training you for that now, at eight. Well, Mattel can kiss my ass, cause that's not happening on my watch.

Now Barbie is a completely different problem for me, and I believe for the self-image of little girls as well. When Barbie is introduced to young impressionable girls, she can quickly become the benchmark for physical beauty. This may impact a young girl's interpretations and beliefs of their own beauty, or lack thereof if they don't feel they share enough, or any, of the physical qualities of Barbie. These qualities include: blonde hair, blue eyes, white skin, and tall thin body. This can be a problem for any little girl, but even more so for little girls of color.

About three years ago, my then five-year-old daughter sat in her room crying. When we went to investigate, she informed us that she was upset because she wasn't as pretty as the other girls at school. We didn't understand where this was coming from. I'm not trying to brag (actually, I am bragging, but saying that I'm not trying to brag makes it seem like I'm not bragging, when the truth is I make pretty babies) my daughter is a very beautiful little girl. Why would she say something like this, and, more importantly, why would she believe something so far from the truth? Now I have to tell you something about men and women. This isn't really about relationships, but you should be used to me going off topic by now, so fuck it.

This is about parenting. Don't worry there will surely be a WTFDYE book on that subject, but for now, I will share this with you. Men and women each have roles to play in parenting. If you cannot accept your role, then your ass needs to be on the pill and wearing two condoms sealed around the base with duct tape, because you sure as hell don't need to have kids. Women, your primary role is to be the nurturer. Simply said, you make sure that your kids are in an environment where they can thrive. Men, your primary role is to be the protector. Simply said, there are a lot of things out there that can hurt a child, including you. Your job is to make sure those things don't hurt your kids. Enough said...for now.

Getting back to my daughter's story. She elaborated that the reason she wasn't as pretty as the other little girls is because they had white skin, and she had brown skin. Those words cut through my side and burned as if I had been struck by Voltron's blazing sword. (Ladies, if you don't get that reference, I blame socialization, anyway you can ask any man between the age of 35 and 49, and they will fill you in). The difference in this case was that Voltron wasn't wielding the sword; it was Barbie. As my daughter's protector, I allowed myself to metaphorically (again, that's a word to substantiate my degree for my momma) be wounded by that skinny bitch, and allowed her to threaten my baby. Fortunately for me, Barbie isn't used to dealing with a man with real balls, so I wasn't down for the count, but instead ready to take Barbie's ass out to protect my daughter. I do want to clarify that I'm not talking about all dolls. I have learned not to be so absolute in life. Raggedy Ann and I have always been cool. And aside from being really creepy, those 18-inch dolls with the blinking eyes can surely be a companion of a child, but if something goes bump in the night, that doll is the first thing going into the fireplace. Just saying, I've seen way too many movies. Nonetheless, the most popular doll in the country is that Barbie doll. This means little girls all over America could be receiving a dangerously wrong message, which plants the first seed of insecurity in their minds.

Now my baby momma, the nurturer, was equal to the task presented by this situation. Remember, she will be focused on the environment and surroundings of her nest. She immediately filled the house with Essence and Ebony magazines so our daughter could see that there is just as much beauty in the brown of her skin as what she believed was monopolized by white skin. Although this tactic helps to establish the understanding that the beauty of women of color is second to none, can we ever be certain how much of the insecurity created by the Barbie factor, actually gets undone?

Unfortunately, and I'm sure unintentionally on the part of my wife; these same magazines tend to present a select few, rare women who have been waxed, painted, air-brushed and personally trained to look like they look. . . So now does this image become the benchmark of beauty in a little girl's mind? Perhaps not just the minds of little girls, but the big ones too. The women in these magazines are correctly identified as "models" because they represent the features and appearance that women are socialized to pursue, or risk not being pretty. And what the fuck do you expect (shameless plug I know) from the trillion-dollar cosmetic industrial complex that pushes make-up, wigs and weaves, padded bras, spanks, wait a minute spanks? Really? If you're fat, get lypo. If you're flat, get 36D's. In fact, 10 billion dollars were spent on cosmetic surgery just last year. This isn't to say that men don't also fall prey to the beast of beauty. There will always be a few metrosexual mitches in the mix; but generally, men are rooted more in vanity, rather than the insecurity that affects women.

I'm surely not suggesting that a woman's insecurity falls completely at the feet of inanimate objects and magazines; I just don't see those things helping the situation.

The Princess & The Pageantry

Once upon a time, in a land far, far away there lived a girl named (insert whatever name you like here, Snow White, Cinderella, Sleeping Beauty, it doesn't matter) who was being treated like shit by some bee- yatch – I mean evil-witch that wanted her dead just because she was so young and pretty.

So let me recap this for all the little girls out there. You are measured by your beauty, so being the prettiest is paramount to your survival. Therefore, you must always compare your own beauty to that of other women, and if you determine that another woman is more beautiful, than you have got to cut a bitch. If you think what I'm saying sounds far-fetched, or you just choose to disagree, that's fine by me. It just lets me know that you obviously don't have cable and haven't seen the Real Housewives of any city where they put two chicks in the same room with each other, just for your viewing pleasure.

So getting back to the story. . . The evil woman, who is afraid that the pretty young girl will inevitably replace her, threatens the pretty little girl's very life and tries to eliminate her.

🕴 *Quick recap. Ok girls, as you age, you need to be constantly vigilant for a younger, prettier woman who could potentially replace you. Once you detect such a woman, then you have got to cut a bitch. Are you starting to see the pattern here?*

If you recall before the commercial break for the recap, the evil woman was about to cut a bitch for being young and pretty, which, in and of itself, is a threat to women everywhere. Let's check out what happens next in our story. The evil woman uses every trick up her sleeve – oh the bitch is crafty – to try to rid herself of the pretty young girl, and she almost has the job done until… (imagine trumpets playing here); the man shows up to save the day. And not just any man, but a charming and handsome Prince who is so taken by the young girl's beauty, that he immediately asks for her hand in marriage, to which she says yes, yes, a thousand times yes. I mean, what little girl doesn't want to be a princess? The birds start to sing, and the animals from the forest frolic and church bells ring throughout the kingdom. There is going to be pomp and circumstance. There is going to be pageantry. There is going to be an event that little girls' dream of their whole lives – a wedding.

So girls, here is what you have to understand more than anything else. You are incapable of saving yourself, and unless you want to be stuck scrubbing your step-mom's toilets or living with horny midgets in the woods, you need to get yourself a man to save you and share his fortune with you. And if you can't find a man...kill yourself*.

The asterisk denotes that this "kill yourself" is covered by the same kill yourself disclaimer, herein referred to as KYD, which has been clearly established and stated earlier in the book and releases the author and publisher from any and all liability should one choose to act upon this kill yourself without first reading the KYD specifically instructing the reader, herein referred to as "yourself" NOT TO kill yourself)!

Where the hell did this whole princess bullshit come from in the first place? Even in their heyday, princesses, like most daughters at the time, were simply pawns used by their fathers to gain advantage for the kingdom, while the sons were an heir to the throne. It must have something to do with that shiny tiara. But is that really enough to make women answer pretentious questions about saving the planet, to perform acts that amount to Letterman's stupid human tricks, and parade around in a swimsuit and pumps? (Who the fuck wears pumps to the beach?) Yes, apparently it is enough. What's even worse is that we throw our babies into these pageants as if it's perfectly normal for little Jon Benet to be dolled up like an adult prostitute. Yeah, daddy's little princess is pretty much the same as pimp my daughter. Sadly ladies, it doesn't matter if you agree with that or not. The fact is, this is what men have made reality, and exactly why men must not be trusted. Only kidding, well slightly kidding, but you do have to realize that this mentality has been established years ago by our founding fathers. That's right, fathers, white men of power that, in their moment of declaring independence, viewed women and blacks as nothing more than property. This has led to generations of suffering and struggle for women. Struggle for the right to work, the right to vote, the right to own property, and the right for equal pay still elude women to this day. James Brown said it best. . .

This is a Man's World

The one value that men have attributed to women is that of an object, a physical object, a sex object. A woman is indoctrinated into a society where her worth is directly proportionate to her beauty and sex appeal. So ladies, make sure you are fuckable, or you're fucked. And what that does to the mentality of a woman is make her feel worthless if she is less than pretty, or if she is "good looking," then she feels compelled to take selfies with her tits and ass hanging out so she can compete against other like-minded – and I used minded loosely – women on some social network. Sure, there are those women who attempt to make the argument that the latter is a display of female empowerment, strong women unapologetically taking ownership of their own sexuality. Well yo ass ain't Gloria Steinem, so put some clothes on and stop pimping yourself to men.

I know this message won't get through to certain women; I mean your ass cheeks have so many followers and likes, that I have to be just another hater, right? At the end of the day, clearly those Facebook likes are the true reliable determination of your self-worth. I'll be the first to admit that suitable visual stimulation is a vital component for habitual masturbation, and therefore, a significant contribution to society. So, thanks, I guess? However, if you look at it with, oh I don't know—thought, you may ask what causes a woman to present herself in that fashion. What are the psychological factors that lead to this choice of self-representation? I mean I get why the chick on the magazine cover or the music video does it; some dude has paid her for her uhhhhhh services. It's a professional relationship similar to that of the prostitute because, sex sells. . . to men.

What happens to a society where men have communicated, through their practices and their policies, that what they value most in a woman is their half or fully naked display? Over time, women start to buy into this bullshit and believe this actually represents their worth or their potential. Please do not misinterpret my meaning. I am not passing judgement of what is right or wrong. Furthermore, this is a generality not an absolute. There are plenty of women who do not subscribe to this behavior. Hopefully, my daughter will be one of them, and thank God for Michelle, Sasha and Malia, oh and you too Oprah. (told ya'll I ain't trying the play with Oprah) I'm just saying that all of the shit that is put on women by a male-dominated society cultivates insecurity. AND NO ONE CAN FUCKING BLAME WOMEN FOR IT! Ike Turner is dead.

CHAPTER EIGHT

Men Aren't From Mars, They're Just Dumb.

So before you start to think I'm biased against women because I am a card-carrying member of the penis club, take a second look at the title of this chapter. That's right! Out of the mouth, rather the keyboard, of a man. Men are dumb! Now before we get into what exactly this means, I have to explain to you the difference between stupid and dumb, so you can understand my choice of words and not mistake my intent. Stupid is a choice generally made by people who have some semblance of intelligence, but nonetheless, inexplicably choose to do, or say, things that could, dare I say should, end in an ass whuppin'. If not an ass whuppin', stupidity will at least incur the reflexive of "what the f@#k did you expect"... the more emphatic "that's what yo ass gets." Just to be clear, men are completely capable of being stupid, but we are inherently dumb. Dumb, unlike stupid, is a condition that causes men to have limited emotional or mental capacity despite not having any physiological disability. The result is that men from time to time will do things that closely resemble something stupid, but differ from stupidity because they were done completely in the absence of actual thought. Ladies, you have to be selective when asking a man what he thinks, because in many instances, his dumbass isn't thinking at all. I'm sorry that's not completely true, I should be more specific here. In most cases he isn't thinking about anything you care about – at all.

Little girls aren't the only ones challenged by society's subliminal subterfuge; that's alliteration; the thing with all the s words; that's called alliter— never-mind. If the last chapter underscored that the treatment of little girls, though unintended perhaps, is harmful, then the signal sent to little boys is …well dangerous.

One Nation, Under. . .

Man is undoubtedly the most dangerous species on the planet. I'm not being excessive in that statement; I'm also not using the term man as a generic term for the species. I mean man, men, males (specifically white men, but we'll save race for another book), and the driving force behind it isn't the desire to be pretty. No, for men it's much more misguided. Men – want to be gods. I know. I know. It sounds absurd, because it is absurd. I acknowledge it, because I lived it. You know what else it is? Dumb. Men are dumb. I'm just saying, if you ask a little girl what she wants to be, and she says a princess, as far-fetched as that may be, it is at least in the realm of possibility. You know what a little boy wants to be. . . fucking Spider-Man. Like that shit could happen. If it isn't Spider-Man, then it's some other super human. And you know why, because being human isn't special enough. We find it limiting, thus spoke Zarathustra. (alright, I know I will need to cite the reference on this one. So I'm in college studying philosophy, long story short Friedrich Nietzsche bitches). Being human is limiting for men because we must acknowledge that there are rules, and more importantly that those rules do apply to us. We don't like that, and many men don't accept it. Why? Because as young boys we are supplied by society with an endless amount of allusions to a limitless existence. (Just a quick side note, if English isn't your first language, or you suffer from re-vitiligo, there will be limits on your limitlessness.) Think about it. The man of steel is not only faster than a speeding bullet, but more powerful than a locomotive. It isn't just comic books either. Take a second, and take a closer look at your religion. Do you see who is parting the sea? . . Moses is. Who is saving humanity and all the animals from global floods. . . Noah is. And the ultimate limit-defying act, raising people and yourself from the dead. . . all men. The greatest biblical feat of a woman, was giving birth to the aforementioned death defying Jesus, and they didn't even let her get laid. I'm not knocking religion, well at least not intentionally at the moment, I'm just saying there's a reason that the bible is the King James version, and that reason is exactly the same as why no one has ever studied *her*-story in school. The best way to deify yourself is to control the narrative that will be passed down for all time. Men control that narrative, and that is why it's called history.

Okay, I admit that may not actually be why it's called history, but it is more logical than believing men (particularly un-pigmented men) are the only humans that have accomplishments worthy of historical, even greater, biblical recognition. That line of reasoning isn't reasonable at all. It's just, well…dumb. Yet, do you know who believes it to be true? It's the penis population of the world, because men are dumb. Men don't want to be beautiful. Make no mistake, it would be great to look like Brad Pitt or Idris Elba, but the truth is, Jay-Z is married to Beyonce. The brotha's flow is phenomenal, but he isn't the prettiest beau at the ball. I don't say this as a dis, and I'm not trying to throw shade. Believe me, I understand that he could record the sound of his own farts and sell more copies of it, than I may ever sell of this book. However, he represents the essence of this particular point about men. His name isn't Jay or Z; it's Shawn. The cat hustled and worked his ass off to get to where he is today because he is driven by what I'm telling you most men are driven by. That is why when he feels the need to re-introduce himself, it isn't as Shawn. Hell, it isn't even as Jay-Z. It's as Hov. (For the hip-hop impaired, the moniker is a reference to Jehovah, which in some religions is the name of God. Although if I were you, I wouldn't take it as there being any chance that Jay-Z will be knocking on your door first thing Saturday morning.) Men want to be gods. They want to live beyond the shackles of this human existence, but to believe, (and men do believe) that it could be possible is just dumb. . . . and dangerous, but mostly dumb.

The Ruler is Back

I want to pick up my earlier point that men don't like to acknowledge that there are rules. Why? It's simple. The acknowledgement of rules would mean that rules also apply to them. So to overcome this nagging flaw in basic transitive logic, men have inherently taken the liberty to create rules, and at the same time, refuse to accept that the rules apply to them. To make it even more hilarious, or pathetic depending on the particular rule, when called out for this hypocrisy, men rationalize the dumb shit as a lapse in judgment or spiritual weakness. Think about it. We all have seen the press conference with a man standing in front of a microphone with his extremely embarrassed and pissed-off wife standing behind his right shoulder in a public show of support. He opens his mouth and asks for what? That's right, he asks forgiveness for his lapse in judgement and moment of spiritual weakness. The reality is that most men believe that their dumb asses will get away with breaking whatever rule they want, particularly if it's a gender-based rule.

Men love making rules for women and, apparently for some men, who like women, love other men.

That's a reference to gay men. Yeah, I know it is referred to as the LGBT, Q,R,S,L,M,N,O,P community, but one thing that really gets the rule-making men worked up, is gay men.

They say dumb shit like, "It was Adam and Eve, not Adam and Steve." However, we never hear them say. "It was Adam and Eve, not Ada and Eve." Of course not, for those dumb asses, Ada and Eve would be hot. And the one screaming the loudest about what the rule should be, always seems to be the dumb fuck caught sucking dicks in airport bathrooms. It seems like all their "glory hallelujahs" turn into "glory holes I blew ya". Isn't that right Senator.

I don't mean to take this on a whole political rant, so I am just gonna throw some words out there, and you can draw the conclusions for yourselves. Abortion rights, contraceptive rights, equal pay rights, fucking rights...oops. That one slipped, wasn't supposed to bring that one up until later. Let's just pretend you didn't read that last one. All the above are rules established by men, that don't even apply to men, so they are unencumbered by the requirement to follow them. It's a pretty slick trick, not out of blatant hypocrisy, but being blatantly dumb enough to believe they have the right to make these rules in the first place, just because they have the power of the penis.

The Pavlovian Man

When I was in college (it makes my mother feel good when I mention I have a degree) I studied psychology. I was always fascinated by the way people behave, and I wanted to be able to understand it from a more clinical perspective. I would have actually become a psychologist, but at the time I thought "who the fuck wants to listen to other peoples shit all day" then I got married...twice; and had a kid ...twice; oh and of course I started handing out advice about relationships. So now, I listen to other people's shit all day, without the ability to tell them, their time is up and here's your bill. Well, you know what they say – if I only knew then, what I know now, I would have started smoking weed a lot earlier. I'm only kidding. Everyone knows you don't need weed until your kids turn four. Where was I? Oh yeah, psychology. So in my studies I learned about this guy, Pavlov, and his dog. What the class was covering at the time was the topic of conditioning.

🕴 *if you are not familiar with the experiments, too damn bad. Google it. I blame no child left behind.*

What Pavlov did, was conduct experiments with a dog. (*Yeah this is a story of a fast dog, for the dog that chases his tail, will be dizzy. These are clappin dogs, rhythmic dogs, harmonic dogs, house dogs, street dogs, dogs of the world unite*) Sorry about that, sometimes the funk just hits you.

🕴 *For my melanin challenged readers that's a P-Funk reference, you can google it.*

Anyway, what Pavlov did was demonstrate that behavior could be conditioned or learned through the use of associated stimuli. What he uncovered was that the dogs salivated whenever they were fed. Furthermore, this behavior was hard-wired into the dogs, meaning they didn't have to learn to do this, they just did it. What made it more interesting was that he also discovered that because the food was always brought to the dogs by his lab assistant, the dogs would salivate every time the assistant walked into the room, even if there was no food. This demonstrated that the dogs learned to associate the assistant with food, and therefore would salivate when the assistant came into the room.

Now I need to tell you, this is an oversimplification of Pavlov's research, so don't go thinking your ass can be the next Jeopardy champion. However, I make the reference to say what some have said about men for years. Men are dogs. Well actually, men are like dogs, in the sense that they too have hard-wired behaviors. And similar to other dumb animals, men behave in very predictable ways under certain circumstances. One thing we learned from Pavlov's dog is that there is a strong behavioral reaction to a visual stimulus, and the same is true for men. In a manner very similar to the Pavlovian puppies, men are extremely visual by nature, so much so that in many instances a visual stimulus is all that is required to elicit a very predictable reaction.

Let me give you a simple example to which most men and women can relate. A lady, a fairly attractive one at that, is with her man having lunch at a sidewalk cafe. The conversation is flowing, so is the wine, and the food is perfect. Then a woman walks past. Halle Berry perhaps? Not a chance, and it doesn't even take a woman who is that extraordinary. If some other random chick in a tank top with 36 C cup breasts rolls by on skates, this dude will not only look, he may even fixate his gaze on her until she is literally out of sight. Why? Why would he be so insensitive and so rude? .. I told you, it's because he's dumb. Remember I am not saying that men are stupid, but we are dumb because we can be so easily manipulated through visual stimulation. It's the reason every woman knows to have a little black dress and pumps to wear to the club. It's one of the main secrets of Victoria, "Wear these thigh highs and this push up bra, and he'll pay your rent." Women are much more discerning; therefore, they evaluate men on a broader range of qualities, the highest being his ability to provide for her. I'm not sayin' she a gold digga, but she ain't messin' with no broke ------- . Men, on the other hand, are just not that complicated. This is usually why men tend to miss the signs that a chick is insane, and is probably going to damage a significant amount of his valued property

† *Just for the record, insane and crazy are not the same thing; crazy gives you a headache, insane gives you head trauma from a blunt*

object. I'm just saying, don't let her know

where you keep your Xbox or your golf clubs.

Men don't care if a woman is homeless, if she's got a phat ass or nice tits. That's good enough for him. He'll still think about fucking her. We will even excuse a goofy face if the body is tight, and by goofy face, I mean a face like Goofy… garsh Mickey! I guess you can blame it on the alcohol. No it's not the Henny. It's the dummy.

So That's What You Like?

Men are visual creatures, and as such men naturally look for optical stimulation, whether it's sports and action movies for violence or magazines and porn for sex. Even in situations where we know that it is an optical illusion or well beyond our reach, for us, the illusion is still enough to make us salivate. This is why porn only works if the people in the movie are visually appealing. Trust me, sales on porn videos with fat ass, toothless, hairy women aren't doing as well as a Kim Kardashian sex tape.

And I do mean fat ass in contrast to phat ass, which is the good phat, not the bad fat, kinda like how HDL is the good cholesterol or how Jam Master Jay is not bad meaning bad but bad meaning good, phcka, phcka phcka phcka phcka phcka phcka phcka, bing, phck, bing,phck, phcka, bing. . . there it is.

So, is the fact that men watch porn an indication about the type of women men like? Absolutely, but not in the way you might think. Again, you have to understand how his dumb ass is wired. They say that a man thinks about sex every seven seconds, I disagree. I say men are exposed to stimuli, mostly visual, which elicits a response that initiates sexual thoughts about every seven seconds. See, what men like are scantily clad, glistening, sexy bodies and most of all fucking; and porn supplies as much of those things as he can download for $4.99 a month. Yes, that's what he likes – to look at, but don't let that worry you ladies, there aren't too many men that actually want a porn star wife. I mean Yeesus, oops Freudian slip, Jesus it takes a woman with qualities that are far more substantive for a man to fall in love. I told you men are dumb, I never said we were stupid.

PART IV

RELATIONSHIIPS 201

CHAPTER NINE

Boy Meets Girl

So here we are ladies and gentlemen, the dream we all dreamed of, boy versus girl in the world series of love. On one side a crazy, insecure woman. On the other side a horny, dumb-ass man. What could be better than to get these two together, if for no other reason than the laughs? All kidding aside, the biggest reason that relationships don't go so well, is because the two participants have no business being together in the first place. Eventually, they find this out and break up. Unfortunately for many people this occurs after some emotional or financial damage has been done. Finding someone that gives you your chance at relationship happiness can be a daunting task. Well, hopefully your ass has been paying attention enough to understand what you are up against in your pursuit, and how you can give yourself better odds for success. Many people go about this all wrong. They spend their time looking for what kind of person they want. However, in the majority of cases, it isn't what you think you want at all, because you really haven't put much thought into it. Most people are really looking for what they believe they want. We build these ideal attributes in our crazy, horny little minds then set out to find Mr. or Mrs. Right. So you know that there is a problem with this, otherwise I wouldn't be bringing it up.

Every relationship you ever have will always have one common denominator. It's you! This is why in order to find the right relationship for you, you have to start with understanding who you really are as a person. The person that you really are, is the same person that someone else is going to have to love. Once you know who you are, then you can discard the silly-ideal attributes that you created in your mind, and realize that you need to find someone that has the characteristics necessary to put up with your specific shit. So I ask you. Who the fuck are you?

Don't lie! Not to yourself; it isn't worth it. Who are you, really? Are you even real? I know that may seem like a strange question, but some muthafucka's just ain't real. They are fake, phony, fronting, wolves in sheep's clothing. That could be you. If it is, then I have to tell you, your relationships will only last as long as it takes for the people around you to find out that you ain't real.

Generally, when people don't like something about themselves, something they don't want to admit about the way they are, they cover it up. They either hide it away as a skeleton in a closet, or in some cases, they even convince themselves that what is true about them, isn't true. Therefore, you need to take a real good self-examination and understand who you really are. I hope that the person you are is the same as the person you show when it comes to a relationship. This gives anyone you encounter an opportunity to "read the label", and know what they are getting themselves into from the beginning.

It might sound like a joke, but imagine how much easier it would be to find the right relationship if people had labels:

"This *person is warm and considerate, but in certain situations can be petty.*"

That might be someone you are willing to take a chance on, right?

"This *person is irresponsible, bad with finances, and has symptomatically blamed others for their failures.*"

You probably know this person, or worse dated them, and it would have saved your ass a whole lot of time and a couple hundred FICO points if you could have read that one from the beginning.

I know it seems unrealistic, but is it completely out of your control to write your own label. The inscription on the Temple of Apollo at Delphi reads "Know Thyself" (Google it damn it). Here's a little known history fact. I share the same birthday as Shakespeare. I'm not a big fan, but there is one line that always stood out to me. "This above all: to thine own self, be true." Relationships are daunting and require courage, the courage to seek to understand yourself. The *serenity prayer* asks God for *the courage to change the things I can.* The "you" that you bring into a relationship is completely within your control. Can I get an amen?

John & Barbara Sitting In a Tree
K-I-S-S-I-N-G

So unless you are skipping around the book, you read about the types of relationships we can experience and the rules of engagement for those particular relationships. But let's face it. What you really paid your money for is to learn something new or profound about those personal relationships, especially if your relationship situation is represented by:

Your inability to find a good man or a good woman.
I know it's hard out there. Be strong.

You're in a relationship, but something's just not right.
You're either worn down, worn out, or both.

Ok, let's talk about it. You may want to get a pencil and notebook or at least a highlighter. All set? Here we go.

First, I want you to understand how these relationships happen. I don't have anything against online dating (except Craigslist. Those people are just plain weird). I find them to be hilarious: FarmersOnly.com; Christians Mingle; Cougar Life. That shit is hilarious, and it's a joke. When I was discussing creating your own label for the person you really are, I wasn't making that synonymous with creating an online profile. I'm not saying that those sites can't work, but whether you use them or not, you need to review some of the previous chapters to understand better the nature and nurture of who we are as men and women. This way you can embark on your search with a realistic foundation of what's actually out there.

Women have thrown the cliché around for years; "a good man is hard to find," and they are absolutely correct. Here is why that is the case. Ladies get your highlighters ready. A woman cannot find a man; she can only be found by a man. That's right. I said it, and I'll say it again (well type it, but you know what the hell I mean). A woman cannot find a man; she can only be found by a man. While we are here, let me speak on another cliché that sounds good but is messing many people up. It's this "there are plenty of fish in the sea." This concept is fallacious and downright stupid if you know anything about fishing. Do you really want to take something home when all you had to do to catch it was to dangle some phony bait in front of it until one was stupid enough to bite and get caught up on a hook? I see that for plenty of women out there, this fishing technique is their entire Facebook/Instagram strategy. Well, good luck making that shit work for anything beyond f*#cking. That's right. I said it. Yes, there are plenty of fish in the sea, but understand this. You don't want any of those fish for anything truly lasting. Remember, the easiest fish to catch are bottom feeders. Besides, do you know what the hell fish starts to smell like after a few days? Whew!

A woman cannot find a man; she can only be found. Here's how it works ladies and gentlemen, and I will expand on it using nature for the analogy. A man is a hunter, like a big cat. (Cincinnati, Detroit or Carolina, whichever one you choose is ok.) A woman is his prey, and trust me ladies, this is the way you want it. When the cat hunts, it eyes up his prey, sometimes picking it out from within a large herd. The big cat watches, studies, and plans on how best to capture its prey. The cat pursues his prey, and his ability to catch what he desires isn't based on some bait dangling in his face like a hook waiting for some dumb fish. No! It's based on the cat's skill, its cunning, and ferocity. There is passion in the pursuit, primal animal magnetism that drives his desire right up until the moment he pounces. Ladies, if you want to pause here to get a glass of ice water, I understand. Tell me though, isn't that pursuit what you want? Fellas, isn't that how you want it to go down? Of course you do, because this is the way that makes it mean something. This is the way that clearly demonstrates to a woman that a man wants her. And more than anything else, a woman needs to feel that a man wants her. I told you she was insecure. And to my ladies, please understand this. All a man truly has, is being a man. He can't give birth to new life. He can't nurture that life from his own body. You get to be a woman, the bearer of life, and the nurturer of life. He only gets to be a man . . . don't f*#k it up for him!

Act Like a Lady

So I guess the logical question now is, if a woman can only be found, how she can improve the probability of that happening for her. The answer is simple. Act like a lady. Before you even ask, I didn't read the Steve Harvey book. I didn't feel like I was the target market. I didn't see either of the movies.

Not that I have anything against Steve Harvey, although I do miss that high-top, I'm just not part of the targeted demographic. I will say this to his credit though, the phrase act like a lady, was much needed to be re-introduced to this generation. Don't get me wrong. I'm not about to go into some chauvinistic rant about a woman's place or some tired old vaginaphobic shit like that. (Yes, *I made that up*) However, I think the pursuit of acting like a lady has been unwisely cast aside by a significant portion of our generation and replaced by a kind of experimental void, misrepresented as a self-expression, that is leaving many women and young girls confused and exposed.

Whether you are straight or a lesbian, prude or a nasty ho, acting like a lady doesn't diminish your ability to be who/how you are, once you figure that out.

Btw the term "nasty ho" in no way is intended to cast these women in a negative light. I can state without hesitation on behalf of the collaborators of this book, that we love them ho's.

What it does demonstrate, however, is your appreciation for discretion, and that everybody doesn't need to know what is going on in that nasty freaky "smack my ass and pull my hair" mind of yours. Let me tell you why both discretion and acting like a lady are important. When you act like a lady, then you get treated like a lady. Here are the perks that a lady receives that bitches don't:

Ladies don't get called bitches.

Ladies don't get treated like bitches.

Ladies don't have their business in the streets.

Ladies attract men who keep their dirt, away from her door.

Ladies attract men who are willing to rise to her standards. (because she has standards)

Ladies attract men who want to treat her like a lady.

That may not sound like much, but trust me, it is. See, a lady knows how to keep her business, *her* business, instead of out on her Facebook page. Trust me ladies, you want a gentleman. See, when you act like a lady (hopefully, it isn't just an act. #knowthyself) you attract gentlemen. The word gentle is there for a reason just in case you never paid attention. A gentleman doesn't kiss and tell. A gentleman keeps a lady's confidence and protects her honor. A gentleman is attracted to a lady because he knows she will keep what happens between the two of them, between the two of them, and for that level of confidence, he will open doors for you, hold your hand, bring you flowers, and give you the best of him. Most importantly, a gentleman

looks to find a lady, while lesser men just try to holla at some bitches.

Getting To-get-her!

What goes right or wrong in relationships is
not predicated on what men do or what women do.
It always comes down to what men and women do
together, once they actually get together.

A problem that many men face is figuring
out, once they found that special someone, how to-
get-her. Here's the interesting thing about that fellas. Believe it or not, in many cases you have already
met that special person; you probably just didn't
think she was that special at the time. Don't worry,
that's actually a good thing. Why you ask? (You
were asking that right?) Because if there is nothing

special about that person at the time you first meet them, then you will need to put in the time to get to know them better in order to discover what it is that eventually makes them special to you. If the attraction for the relationship is predicated on a visual attribute, then it can only last as long as that, which is visually pleasing, stays pleasing. Ok so you might be having a "what you talking bout Willis" moment, so I suggest you read the last sentence again; I'll wait.

So the moral of the story is this fellas, if the fact that a woman has a big ass or nice tits is what caught your attention and made her special, once those attributes age (and they will) she won't be too special to you anymore. Even worse, she may only be special to you until the next phatter ass and perkier tits come along, next thing you know, you're following some trick you don't even know on Instagram. I know. I know. What's my problem with Instagram? I just think it's the concept of calling people followers connotes that the person being followed is a leader. I just don't know how much leadership comes from a picture of someone's ass. I think I'd be more comfortable if we called those followers what they truly are. . . voyeurs. No offense to these very beautiful women whose fame is derived from the Internet, but Kim and Kanye are not Denzel and Pauletta, and never will be. Can you tell me how many women Denzel was with before Pauletta? or how many men Pauletta was with before Denzel? Of course not, you also have no idea what goes on within their relationship. Because she is a lady, and he is a gentleman. However, I'm sure you can name at least three dudes Kim Kardashian has been with just this decade.

I'm just saying to my brothas out there. Don't be so quick to chase a woman based on what the eyes can see.

Don't worry white guys, there is no race implied in my use of brothas, so yes you are included - this time.

It is extremely important that you put time into the relationship to discover what is truly special about a woman in her mind and heart. If she happens to have a donkey...Jackpot! Nonetheless, it's what you discover about who she really is, that will make her special. It will also be what makes her beautiful in your eyes, always.

I said that in many cases, that special someone is someone you have already met. Ok, so what if she isn't someone you have already met? Then there are some key indicators to look at that will help guide your choices.

1. *Is she effortless?*

This isn't the same as being high maintenance. Hell, you don't even know this woman yet. This is more about the "p" word. Presence, fool! Get your mind out of the gutter. Do you have to attempt to be something or someone you're not in order to be with her, or is she effortless? Can you just be yourself with her? (If you don't know who you are then check your label). How and in what circles does she carry herself? If she's out there, then you will need to be out there as well. If that is not your thing, then take a pass.

The second indicator is contrary to what most people think. Many people say, "you have to look at how a man treats his momma," but that's some stupid ass advice because a man only has one momma, and it ain't you. She brought him in this world; nurtured him, guided him, took him to the zoo, and bought him Christmas toys. No woman compares to her. Just because he treats her well, doesn't have shit to do with how he will treat you. Do you actually think that some pussy you gave him last night can compete with the Sega Genesis his momma bought him when he was fifteen? Hell to the no. That's why there is a woman at the store right now buying an Xbox One for some grown-ass man, cause she is still trying to outdo his momma.

2. *How does a woman treat her mother?*

I know. I know. Right now you're thinking, how does that tell me anything? Well just keep reading. If a woman has no respect for her mother, either in the way she talks to her ,or talks about her, and shows no ability to defer to her mother as the matriarch, FLAG! You don't want to mess with that woman. There are some exceptions, like if her momma ain't shit or is clearly insane; but other than that, if a woman does not defer to her mother's station, she surely won't give a fuck about anything you do or show you any respect the minute that she doesn't feel like it.

3. *How does a woman treat her children?*

This is of course assuming that she has kids. If a woman does have kids, but instead of living with her, they live with another relative – FLAG! If a woman has more than two kids from more than two men – FLAG! If a woman has a child, but the father doesn't support or see the child – FLAG! I'm not saying that you need to avoid these women; they may truly be the kind of woman who had to learn the hard way, and now have it all figured out. Everyone, well maybe not everyone, ok let's go with most people, deserve the opportunity to prove that their past is just that – their past. However, you do need to be mindful of her decision making, because if she is unable to make good decisions when it pertains to her kids, then she won't be able to make good decisions when it comes to you.

🕴 *Just a side note for some of the men out there, and you know who you are. You may be in denial about how jacked up yo shit actually is, but some of you should know that if a woman is trying to kick it with a dude like you, then she makes bad decisions #knowthyself, #fixurlifeup.*

The Sacrifice of Victor

As a society, we always seem so shocked about how many relationships don't work out. When the reality is, we should probably be more amazed that any actually do. Nevertheless, the fact that even one relationship works is enough to give us hope that, perhaps, we too could experience true blissful intimacy. Well stop kidding yourself. I'm not saying that you can't make relationships work.

Hell, I wouldn't have brought you this far just to tell you to give up. However, even when you do make a relationship work, it won't be blissful. In order for it to work, you have to put in a lot of work, hard, seemingly un-appreciated, work with a hefty side dish of sacrifice. It's no accident that I didn't say that it takes love. I subscribe to the Ella Mae Bullock doctrine (that's Tina Turner y'all, and the name of the song is . . . What's Love Got To Do With It)

We discussed love earlier, so we need to keep it in mind that love is an emotion, and though we like to sing songs about love and write stories about love, love is still quite ephemeral. Don't get me wrong. I absolutely believe love is an important accessory to have in a relationship. Yes, I called it an accessory. We just need to acknowledge that as an emotion, love has to be evoked as a response to a stimulus, like a smile, or in some cases, just a memory of a smile. Love isn't what makes a relationship work. Love is more the emotional motivation for us to keep putting in the effort that makes a relationship work.

I mentioned a side dish of sacrifice. Sacrifice, contrary to some erroneous beliefs, does not mean that you are suffering. I blame the Christians. No, I'm joking. . . kind of. We hear the word sacrifice, and we envision this Mel Gibson *"Passion of The Christ"* horror flick and lose sight of the fact that the suffering is what was endured in order to make the sacrifice. Actually, sacrifice simply means to give an offering. A sacrifice isn't a negative thing; it's a gift. In the case of Jesus, the gift was his life. If he had been executed less horrifically, say by lethal injection, the sacrifice would still be the same, but they probably wouldn't have sold as many books. Therefore, when I talk about the sacrifice necessary for a lasting relationship, I'm just saying that you have to willingly give what you have to offer as a gift, then (and this is the hard part) expect nothing in return.

See, I told you this relationship stuff wasn't rocket science. Of course, it rarely works that one person is willing to sacrifice for another. There are too many forces working against the ideal of sacrifice. Self-absorption, secret agendas, or the law of reciprocity! You inherently expect that if you give something of yourself, then you deserve something in return; and that's why yo' ass ain't Jesus.

TTYL.

Until we meet again, Peace, Love, and please. . .pay the f*#k attention!

www.ingramcontent.com/pod-product-compliance
Lightning Source LLC
LaVergne TN
LVHW021447080426
835509LV00018B/2197